"The Bowery—no dainty kid-glove business, but electric force and muscle."
—Walt Whitman, 1888

"What infinite use Dante would have made of the Bowery."
—Theodore Roosevelt, 1914

"C'est le quartier le plus sinistre de la ville."
("It's the most sinister neighborhood of the city.")
—Albert Camus, 1946

"Let's get out of here, it's too literary. Let's get drunk on the Bowery..."
—Jack Kerouac, 1960

THE
BOWERY

A History of Grit, Graft and Grandeur

ERIC FERRARA

Charleston   London

THE
History
PRESS

Published by The History Press
Charleston, SC 29403
www.historypress.net

First published 2011

Manufactured in the United States

ISBN 978.1.60949.178.9

Library of Congress Cataloging-in-Publication Data
Ferrara, Eric.
The Bowery : a history of grit, graft, and grandeur / Eric Ferrara.
p. cm.
Includes bibliographical references.
ISBN 978-1-60949-178-9
1. Bowery (New York, N.Y. : Street)--History. 2. Historic sites--New York (State)--New York. 3. Street addresses--New York (State)--New York. 4. New York (N.Y.)--History. 5. New York (N.Y.)-
-Social life and customs. 6. New York (N.Y.)--Social conditions. 7. New York (N.Y.)--Biography.
I. Title.
F128.67.B6F47 2011
974.7'1--dc22
2010052259

Dedicated to my colleagues at the Lower East Side History Project

Contents

CONTENTS

Foreword

Bums.

Bums and winos, homeless hobos, lying on the sidewalk sleeping it off, sitting up for a moment's blurry wakefulness to coax the bottle upside down and drain it, as if a drop of dregs could fix a drink. Unshaven, unwashed and unashamedly unkempt, spare-a-dime panhandlers wobbling among the flophouses and dives. No stores, no churches, no movies, not even a thrift shop; no pawnshops—nothing to hock; no laundromats, no cleaners; not a barber, not a business, not a warehouse, not even a whorehouse. Just bars and Bowery bums between the lighting wholesalers and the restaurant suppliers. Skid Row. A ghost town, filled with living ghosts, and not long for the living, either. The Bowery.

For as long as living memory, the Bowery meant bums. Up the street or down, on every block of it, that's all you'd see. Nobody else seemed to go there—why would they? There was nothing to buy, nothing to see, nothing to do. And besides, a trip to the Bowery meant being begged for a dime every three minutes, a cigarette every two, as you gingerly stepped over the bodies lying asleep along the sidewalk. It wasn't a pretty picture. Not a dangerous neighborhood—hundreds of artists lived there in cheap commercial loft space, though you'd never know it on a visit; all you'd see were the bums. Not dangerous, no, it was just rock bottom, like an underworld hid beneath the slums, the lost creatures that even the slum refused. At every turn, in every corner and alley, written on every Bowery forehead, every sunken eye in toothless face, *abandon all hope who come here.*

How does a street, lined with handsome old nineteenth-century commercial buildings, a wide thoroughfare expanded for traffic, sandwiched between a once thriving industrial zone to the west, SoHo, and to the east once a densely populated, burgeoning immigrant ghetto—how does a central corridor between business and labor dry out so completely to the bottom of the barrel?

Every ghost town once had its boomtown, before the tumbleweeds rolled by. They rose up like an excited amusement park, brilliant and new and proud, attracting all and every, and all and every business, market and con man is drawn to make a killing on the gathered crowd. But few boomtowns were ever so spectacular, so varied, so busy and bright as the Bowery once was. The Bowery was no remote boomtown in a western desert; it was the boomtown amidst the biggest city in all America. It was the brazen, blazing boom of New York City.

Equally home to opera and burlesque, museums and saloons, hotels and brothels, gangsters and gays, the Bowery had catered to every taste. In the nineteenth century, it had been not only the city's theater district—with the largest theaters in America—but also the daytime commercial district, its nightlife district and red-light district, its center of political power through the gangsters quartered in the Bowery saloons—in short, it was the city's heartbeat.

Bowery street walls were covered with advertisements hawking every ware for the passing street parade. Business owners conceived the notion of lighting up the signs with gas lamps, the nineteenth-century predecessor of neon and Times Square light boards, decades before Times Square yet existed. The Bowery was known far and wide as America's brightest street, brighter than the Champs-Elysées, so they said.

Unlike the severe English Puritan Protestant heritage of the rest of America, New York, with its frank mercantile legacy, enjoyed lively nightlife and theater. And like a great street of a continental European capital, the Bowery, too, boasted grand opera and trenchant theater. The German immigrants held opera at the Bowery Theater and, just across the way, the Bowery Amphitheater. The Irish, always highly politicized, staged melodramas with the strapping Irish hero foiling the villain, unmistakably dressed as the Protestant elite—black top hat, slender black suit and dark coat or cloak—the Protestant overlord who owned the city, who owned industry, who underpaid his Irish labor and preyed on the Irish women thrown on the streets, selling themselves to feed their kids and meet the exorbitant rents demanded by the same slender black-suited Protestant landlords. Theater was integral to the city's self-identity, and the Bowery flaunted its social character in high relief through its spectacles and drama. The Bowery loudly voiced the swelling ranks at the broad foundational bottom of industrial muscle, the driving engine of the new city and the new country.

It all began with a modest Native American footpath and a little village of farms.

When the Dutch set up their outpost of the West India Company—New Amsterdam was not a colony of Dutch sovereignty but merely a company trading post—they found a trail extending from the southernmost shore running steadily north, looping around the taller hills, extending all the way to the other end of the island. It was a convenient and natural path, eventually widened into a wagon road. It became the site of New York's first African village.

The Dutch were here to trade, and the big trade of the day was the slave trade. Africans had been brought to New Amsterdam within a year of the first settling in 1625. But the Dutch were liberal toward their slaves: after taking eighteen or twenty of the best years of their lives, and no doubt not caring to feed them into old age, the Dutch would afford their slaves a kind of conditional freedom. The freed could even own their own land, but their services could be demanded in emergencies, and their children would remain slaves.

Besides conditional freedom and ownership, Africans had recourse to protection as well. The Dutch, being a mercantile breed, cherished a strong juridical system. Property, contracts and business deals all require robust, sound courts and firm respect for rule of law. Moreover, the Dutch valued the freedom borne of justice, since back in the Old World they had spent one hundred years of warfare to free themselves from the Spanish Hapsburgs and the Holy Roman Empire. Freedom and tolerance made good business sense, trademark of the independent middle-class Dutch burgher. The local Africans in New Amsterdam took good advantage. Three slaves sued their owners to pay them for their work. True justice is blind: they won.

If this doesn't look like Uncle Tom and Simon Legree on the plantation, it wasn't. But it wasn't equality either. In 1643, Dutch records show that two free Africans were given farm lots on either side of this path, by then a "double wagon" road. It seems likely that the Dutch gave these particular lots along the Lenape trail in order that the Africans would form a buffer zone in case the natives got restless and the Lenape came marching down the literal warpath, as in fact they did. When the Dutch traded firearms for beaver skins up north in the trading post that would become Albany, and the local governor of New Amsterdam prohibited the sale of firearms to the local Lenape, the ill will between the two cultures of the island wouldn't hold much longer. Squeezed now between Mohicans and Dutch, the Lenape gnawed on their log of gripes, as they lost their hunting grounds to clearings opened for permanent structures, clearings slowly creeping along to the north and east and west, steadily driving away their wildlife. They saw their future dwindle, the horizon of their freedom clouded and darkened. The Dutch, anticipating violence, struck first, hoping to teach the tribe a lesson. But as with all wars and all quarrels, the first strike was just the start, soon to be followed by much worse trouble than any strike might have intended to prevent.

A buffer zone surrounding the Lenape trail was a tactical solution. Within a couple of decades, these lots had multiplied into a little African village, the first African village in New York. By 1670, a couple of Dutch, visiting the now English colony, came upon this village, full "of blacks and mulattoes and whites," as they wrote in their account. The village was called the Bouwerij Village; in English, "the Farm Village." It was the beginning of the Bowery.

And so Domingo Antony and a widow, Catelina Antony, the two free Africans who first were given lots by the double-wagon road, had set themselves to seeding and tilling the ground for the future of a road they could never have dreamt in their pastoral world of seasonal crops and domestic animals, one-story houses and wooden barns, glum and testy natives, fierce winters, humid summers and white folks and their rule.

Two hundred years later, a young journalist living in Brooklyn ferried over to Manhattan to knock about the Bowery, his favorite street in the city. Contemning all pretensions, drawn to the vigor of ordinary hardworking men, he admired the rough-and-tumble Irish b'hoys—the local gang members—and men working in their shirtsleeves. In the evening, he'd take in a play at one of the many Bowery theaters to see one of the great Shakespeareans at mid-century, Edwin Booth or Edwin Forrest. Fifty years later, when Walt Whitman had become the poet of the American spirit, he remembered his years as a journalist enjoying the Bowery, where he'd found plain human nature unadorned and unbuttoned, and throngs of it. The Bowery drew crowds to express their unmediated desires, the exuberance of entertainment and sex. That was the stock in trade of the Bowery, built by desire, expressing it everywhere and selling satisfaction.

The Bowery that Whitman saw was the unintended effect of one structure: the Bowery Theater. Built as a distinguished venue for the elite, its managers quickly recognized that the real money lay elsewhere with the vast working public, with its eager and immediate hunger. Within a decade, the Bowery Theater exchanged the delicate sensibilities of gentility for blackface minstrelsy and melodrama, opera and Shakespeare, always popular with their exaggerated villains and third acts strewn with the dead.

Theater was working-class entertainment. If you were wealthy, you had a piano in your parlor. A young eligible bachelor of means and fine pedigree might visit to accompany young Gertrude singing of an evening soiree as the onlookers contemplated the suitability of their match—that was entertainment. For the rest of New York, mostly immigrants brought here as cheap labor for the city's burgeoning industry and living in tenements with no parlors but packed with boarders like sardines (and smelling like it—there was no running water, much less baths), whole families of boarders to meet the rent, theater was the getaway from the domicile, such as it was. Theaters were as popular as the movies are today, but the audience went there not just to see the story and the spectacular stage effects—the Bowery Theater once replaced its stage with a huge pool and floated a ship for a pirate fantasy. They went as much to be in a crowded place, close to everyone they knew, the largest crowds anywhere anyone could gather. They went to find their friends, drink with them in the theater, carouse with them, challenge their rivals, abuse the actors on the stage, catcall at one another, threaten one another, fight with one another, maybe even riot. Entertainment wasn't waiting properly and obediently for the curtain of the first act to applaud. The audience was as active as the stage and more volatile. When Thomas Daddy Rice created the blackface role of Jim Crow for the Bowery Theater, white audiences were so aroused by the abuse they saw in it that they jumped onto the stage, enthusiastically crowding around the dancer, until the stage could hold no more. At a time long before the political demonstration, Bowery political leaders harnessed that volatility by orchestrating political riots in and around the theaters as the sound box of vox populi.

Success breeds imitation, and the success of the Bowery Theater was no exception. The Bowery Amphitheater opened just across the street, featuring similar popular fare: minstrelsy, opera, dance competitions. The beginnings of tap dance grew out of these competitions between the local Irish and local blacks performing on stage in a fury of athleticism lasting for hours. German management eventually bought the Amphitheater and devoted it to the German immigrant public, of which there was plenty: New York was the third-largest German-speaking city in the world, after Vienna and Berlin.

In short order, the Bowery became New York's theater district, and along with it came the nightlife district, the entertainment district, the hotel district, the red-light district, the underground gangster lair, corruption, graft, crime and with those, above all, politics.

Politics of New York in the nineteenth century reflected the irony of industrialism. Industry required cheap labor and lots of it. By bringing desperate immigrants from every corner of the Old World, industry had brought into its home its most dangerous enemy: a vast voting working-class public. The island owned by Protestant elites was, by mid-century, run by a largely Catholic working-class constituency. In particular, the Irish gangs organized Tammany Hall, the political club that ran the Democratic Party. Candidates and caucuses and voting booths were all controlled by gangs. Their influence did not end at the election. Corruption and extortion became the standard practice of city politics. The gangs were quartered in their saloons, and the saloons lined the Bowery.

Maybe the greatest of Bowery pols was Big Tim Sullivan. Like the typical Tammany Hall man, he was a reformer and benefactor of the working class. And typical, too, he was closely connected to the gangs. The Sullivan Law, requiring licenses for all sorts of concealed weapons, allowed him to disarm and imprison his enemies and license his allies. The effect of the law was not to control gangsterism but to expand it.

Integral to the economy of the Bowery, and of the entire city, was prostitution. No mere byproduct of poverty, it was all but a planned consequence of the wage structure. Industrialists would not afford a living wage, throwing immigrant women onto the streets to sell themselves to those very same industrialists and their sons. It was a marriage of convenience, their bodies owned and their homes too. Their illicit and their licit wages reverted immediately to the landlords, again, the same Protestant elites who owned the city's industry. They had them coming and going. The beginning of the labor movement arose out of a degree of exploitation that we scarcely remember and can no longer imagine.

Theater owners encouraged the construction of whorehouses next door—it was good for business. But the audiences needn't travel so far as next door: every Bowery theater employed "waitresses" selling more than just the peanuts the buyers would chuck at the actors they didn't like. A john might take a waitress up to the third balcony reserved for the purpose—no need to find a room. When the city finally cracked down on public prostitution, the waitresses were prohibited and the third balcony was renamed the "Family Circle." Some theaters today still offer the Family Circle as the cheapest seats in the house. Clever managers found means to skirt the law, which defined a theater as a raised stage with a curtain. They removed the curtains and kept the "waitresses," and now we call it "cabaret." Money is the father of invention.

Theater managers were not alone among scammers on the Bowery. There were many, and they were colorful: Madam Prewster, an early psychic, set up a business as a panderer, using her predictions to unite unsuspecting immigrant girls with callow young men looking for a cheap fling. Like Stephen Crane's Bowery gal Maggie, the girls would have a brief moment of fun and excitement, anticipating an idyllic future with a husband of worth, followed with ruin by abandonment and likely a life of prostitution.

Perhaps the greatest scammer of all time and the inventor of marketing and the business of scamming, P.T. Barnum got his start on the Bowery in 1835 with Joice Heth, purportedly 161 years old, whom he billed as George Washington's own nanny. At her death, the pathologist pronounced her no older than 80. Barnum had displayed her at Chatham Square at the southernmost end of the Bowery. She was a wild success, partly through his intimations that Heth might be a hoax, which aroused even more curiosity. It was an audacious ploy and an auspicious entry into the world of what he liked to call "hokum" or, as we call it today, "advertising."

In the 1890s, scamming turned serious in the saloons, where waiters would slip knockout drops—carbolic acid—into their patrons' drinks and then bring them to the basement and roll them for all their possessions. At McGurk's saloon, nested in a cheap hotel full of prostitutes on their last leg, the desperate girls would steal the carbolic acid for a final solution to their unhappiness, giving McGurk's saloon the name "Suicide Hall."

As the city expanded north and new, non English–speaking immigrants moved into the neighborhoods surrounding the Bowery, the focus of nightlife in New York began to shift from the Bowery to the Tenderloin. When Yiddish theater occupied the Bowery halls, English-language theater looked for newer venues in more respectably anglicized districts. The construction of the elevated train over the Bowery, with its noise and smoke, didn't help. It literally and figuratively cast a shadow on the street. Although the Bowery continued to develop through the 1890s, the profile of the street had altered. It was known as a dangerous street, a dark corner not only for gangs and gamblers but also for marginals, for "fairies"—several gay bordellos opened on the Bowery—and for the estranged. The *Times* relished stories of apparent paupers who, upon their demise, were discovered to have been immensely wealthy but alienated from their families, having come to the Bowery seeking the anonymity of a street that never asked questions. One young scion of a wealthy San Francisco family followed an actress across the country only to die in a Bowery flophouse, leaving the brief suicide note, "I lived and died for love." The desperate and isolated had found the Bowery.

In the twentieth century, as America's skid row, the Bowery's fame was eclipsed by the image of poverty and desperation of the indigents whom even the slums rejected. Yet throughout its worst years it housed hundreds of artists drawn to the abandoned commercial lofts and the alternative character of the place, set apart from the mainstream. The list of artists who lived on the Bowery is a litany of the greatest and most respected names in visual arts of the twentieth century.

Poverty drove development away from the Bowery for nearly a century. There are a few Depression-era structures on the Bowery, but after the 1940s construction ended there completely, while the rest of New York grew by leaps and bounds. Neglect and abandonment buried the Bowery like the volcanic ash of Pompeii, preserving the history untouched.

The Bowery is not just the oldest thoroughfare in New York, deeply entrenched in our city's collective character, myth and lore, not just Whitman's haunt and Crane's, Foster's and Burroughs's, not just the birthplace of New York's original theater traditions of minstrelsy and Jim Crow, Irish Mose and Yiddish Shmendrick, vaudeville and burlesque. It's not just the turf of the b'hoys and the gangs, shoulder-hitters and Tammany pols who ran New York out of their saloons, nor just the skid row of flophouses, whorehouses and dives. Along with its colorful and influential past, the Bowery is also the most architecturally and historically diverse street in the city, comprising buildings from nearly every decade between 1800 and 1940, an indispensable resource of two centuries of American architectural design, as well as a repository of social, economic, political, immigrant, labor, underground, criminal, deviant, marginal, countercultural, literary, musical, dramatic and artistic history.

When development in New York slowed and the city declined into bankruptcy, as it suffered white flight and the loss of its tax base to the suburbs, the neighborhood to the west of the Bowery took advantage of the hiatus to protect Little Italy, including part of the west side of the Bowery. The east side of the Bowery, belonging to the Lower East Side and stigmatized as a slum, was given no such protection. Community District 2, including the wealthy neighborhoods of SoHo, Greenwich Village and the West Village, continues to promote preservation with historic designations over nearly three-quarters of its land area. It has managed to protect now the entirety of the west side of the Bowery with either special zoning or historic district landmark designations. Community District 3, the old Lower East Side, has succeeded in protecting exactly one block of Stuyvesant Street. The entire east side of the Bowery is open to high-rise hotel and condo development. It is being demolished and redeveloped as I write.

The history of the east side of the Bowery is long. The pre-1830 town houses at 135, 141, 151 and 173 are among the oldest structures in New York. Klein Deutschland survives in the Germania Fire Insurance building, German meeting halls like Steuben House and the Germania Bank's several locations. Labor unions met in halls all along the Bowery, and labor history was made at 263, the Journeyman Bakers' International Union, which organized in 1869 the largest union demonstration the city had seen.

There were political halls—Horace Greeley delivered a powerful speech in support of U.S. Grant's candidacy at a Seventeenth Ward Republican meeting at 327 in 1868—and political saloons. Farley's, at 133, poured ale to Tammany from 1885 until 1915. There were curiosity "museums" (Worth's at 101), burlesque "concert halls" (197) and notorious gangster dives (Geoghegan's, 105), all of which still stand; only the theaters, once the Bowery's hallmark, are gone, some of the greatest only recently demolished.

The turn-of-the-century decline toward skid row, hideaway of the destitute, the criminal and the estranged, is reflected in the missions—Salvation Army and the Bowery Mission (still operating)—and the flophouses (slowly disappearing). Yet despite its decline, the Bowery still boasts old buildings of dignity, grace and beauty in every American style: Federal, Greek Revival, Italianate, Neo-Grec, Romanesque, Renaissance Revival, Queen Anne, Beaux Arts, Art Nouveau and Art Deco, and even rarities unique to the Bowery that defy category.

This rich fabric cannot be replaced or reproduced. Until recently it survived largely through neglect. Renewed interest in the Bowery, far from protecting its treasures and its unique context, threatens to erase them forever, replacing them with a single new, uniformly twenty-first-century ahistorical context.

Some developments on the Bowery reflect an effort to fit into the historical context of the street, but most are designed without any thought of place or community. These developments no longer reflect urban design. The developers of the Cooper Square Hotel, toward the northern reach of the Bowery, could easily have placed their open-air party space facing Cooper Square itself, one of the widest squares in the city and a commercial, not a residential, area. No one would have noticed or cared. Instead, they placed their noise area on narrow Fifth Street facing a senior facility. When Gwathmey-Siegel designed the base of its novel and beautiful all-glass Sculpture for Living at Astor Place, it included only one storefront, a bank, offering nothing to the neighborhood but a single flat glass wall. The Scarano development on Fourth Street drops all pretensions. It advertises its driveway as "gated," thinly disguising the intent to protect the residents from the enemy: the neighborhood.

Development no longer strives to create ideal neighborhoods. It follows the developer's easiest, fastest buck. And when an early town house is nominated for landmarking, the owner is likely to demolish it immediately, legally or not, before its development potential is frozen by law.

Real estate has always been the Gargantua in New York, eating its own young in a perpetual cycle of cannibalism, a Saturn that sees and desires only the present for the sake of today's fresh money, indifferent to its past. Built structure is our history visible. So whoever owns property owns history, and redevelopment carelessly erases history off the face of the streetscape, leaving the raw value for profiteers, living who knows where. City administration colludes.

Bums.

Rob Hollander

Opposite: Northerly view of Bowery from Canal Street/Confucius Plaza. *Courtesy of Shirley Dluginski and Mitchell Grubler.*

Preface

It would take volumes of books to do a topic such as the Bowery justice. I have chosen to explore but a small, diverse sampling of some of the lesser-known addresses and stories that shaped the character (and legends) of this great thoroughfare.

Broadway gets all of the glory, but this underappreciated avenue played a vital role in the cultural, economical and political development of our city. I hope this publication helps put the Bowery's historic role into perspective and inspires further research.

Chapter 1

Introduction

LENAPEHOKING

When the officers of the Dutch West India Trading Company settled Manhattan Island in the seventeenth century, they navigated the same centuries-old trails carved by the soles of Native American peoples over generations. Only one trail existed that ran the entire length of Manhattan Island, and it began just steps from the walls of Fort Amsterdam. The Dutch referred to the path as the Wickquasgeck Trail because it led to the northern territories of the Wickquasgeck Indian, who lived in today's Bronx and Westchester region.

Less than a mile north of Fort Amsterdam, the Wickquasgeck Trail would veer to the east of a body of water the Dutch called Kalck-Hook or Kolck (a probable reference to the piles of empty oyster shells found there) and continue northeast over a hill said to be used by native hunters to survey small game in the marshy lowlands below. The earliest settlers would picnic atop this hill, gazing down over cherry orchards and across the great river Hudson sailed a century prior. The air was crisp and sweet with the smell of fruits and ocean. Early accounts state that thick flocks of birds could block out the sun, and it was sometimes impossible to hold a conversation over the squeaks, chirps and rumblings of the lush wildlife.

Bear, deer, wolves, beaver and hundreds of bird and fowl species were the earliest residents of Lower Manhattan, as were the Lenape peoples,

Early photo of native trail from the Inwood section of Manhattan Island. *From* Indian Paths in the Great Metropolis, Part 1, *by Reginald Pelham Bolton; photo by W.L. Calver.*

an Algonquin society whose name can be translated to "Real People" or "Original People." The Lenape had inhabited Manhattan Island for one thousand years by the time Peter Minuit famously "purchased" the island in 1626.

The territory of the Lenape, referred to as Lenapehoking, covered a vast portion of the Northeast between Pennsylvania and Connecticut. According to *Native New Yorkers: The Legacy of the Algonquin People of New York* by Evan T. Pritchard, the Lenape may have called Manhattan Island *E-hen-da-wi-kih-tit*, while the Mohawk (another Algonquin society) referred to it as *Knonoge* ("Place of Reeds"). Noted ecologist and author

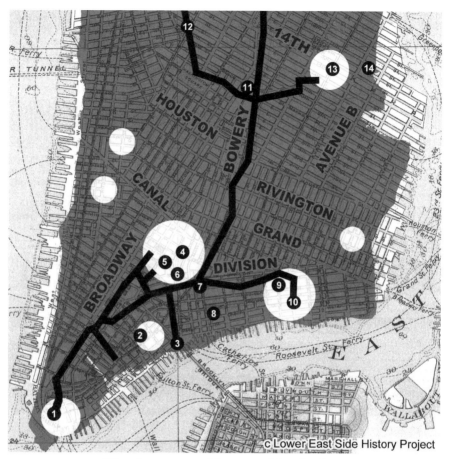

The Lenape of Lower Manhatan

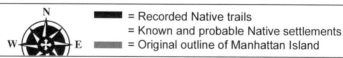

= Recorded Native trails
= Known and probable Native settlements
= Original outline of Manhattan Island

1 - Kapsee/Canoe landing
2 - Natural water source
3 - Canoe landing
4 - Werpoes Village
5 - Collect Pond
6 - Planting fields
7 - Lookout hill (Chatham Square)

8 - Cherry orchard
9 - Natural water source
10 - Rechtanck/Canoe landing
11 - Kintekoying
12 - Trail to Sapohanikan
13 - Planting fields
14 - Canoe landing

Courtesy of Lower East Side History Project, based on data from the Wildlife Conservation Society's Mannahatta Project, NYC Oasis project and recorded Dutch accounts.

Eric W. Sanderson, among others, claims that the natives called the island *Mannahatta* ("Island of Many Hills"), while others believe the original Lenape names have been lost forever.

The Dutch referred to one of the largest Lenape communities on Manhattan Island as "Werpoes." It was situated on the banks of the Kalck-Hook, a natural spring water collect that has nurtured an abundance of life since Manhattan was carved away by retreating glaciers at the end of the ice age. The pond was shielded by two mighty hill ranges to its west and north, rising well above one hundred feet (higher than any twentieth-century tenement building). The east was the previously mentioned "picnic hill" (rising about thirty feet above sea level) and the Wickquasgeck Trail, which connected Werpoes to several smaller villages and native sites. Hundreds of Lenape are presumed to have lived at Werpoes, which is buried deep beneath today's Chinatown.

It was most likely the people of Werpoes who made the deal with Minuit, but by that time, only a couple of hundred Lenape remained on the island anyway. European settlement had an almost instant effect on the native population; foreign diseases decimated entire villages, and the introduction of alcohol broke down communities from the inside. Resulting wars (and massacres) would further diminish the native population, and by the 1640s, many who stayed behind were trading with or working for the Dutch in some capacity.

By 1626, the "picnic hill" would be marked for settlement (a livestock farm) and several company plantations—or *bouwerijs*—were mapped out along the Lower Wickquasgeck Trail, becoming the first major European development on Manhattan Island outside of Fort Amsterdam. These farms were prepared to provide sustenance for incoming settlers.

Some of the very first nonnative residents along the Bowery were black—slaves, indentured workers and freemen given land for various reasons, most importantly to act as a buffer between Fort Amsterdam and warring natives. Some freed blacks would prosper, but many would not be successful under harsh conditions. Regardless, the area would attract a large black population by the end of the century. According to *Root & Branch: African Americans in New York & East Jersey, 1613–1863* by Graham Russell Hodges, a district west of the Bowery and south of Astor Place was referred to as "Negro Land."

In 1660, Bouwerij Village was established to the east of the Wickquasgeck Trail under a portion of today's East Village, on the property of Governor Petrus Stuyvesant. According to accounts, several

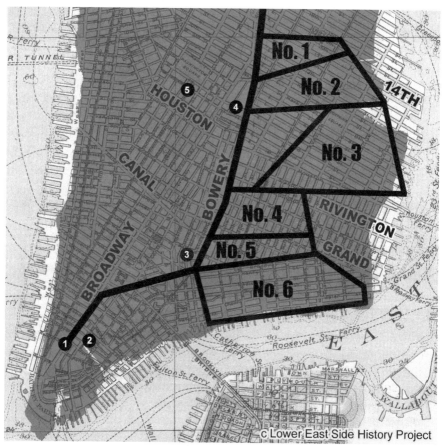

Original Bouwerij Boundaries & Black Populations

= Approximate estate boundaries
= Original outline of Manhattan Island

1 - Fort Amsterdam gate
2 - Dutch West India slave compound
3 - Freed slave farm
4 - Freed slave farm
5 - Freed slave farm

Courtesy of Lower East Side History Project.

freed blacks lived in the small community alongside Europeans and others (including up to forty of Stuyvesant's slaves). At this time, the Lower Wickquasgeck Trail between modern-day Union and Chatham Squares would come to be known as Bouwerij Road, and the legacy of the Bowery was seeded. It would remain the only major road in and out of the city for the next century and a half.

On August 27, 1664, the residents of New Amsterdam awoke to a flotilla of menacing British warships anchored in New York Harbor. Without a single gunshot, Governor Stuyvesant handed over control of New Amsterdam to the English, who would go on to rule Manhattan Island almost consecutively for over a century. The foundation of a city that the Dutch had laid would grow exponentially under direction of the British. New York was taking baby steps toward becoming an international center of commerce—with Lower Manhattan as its heart and the old Wickquasgeck Trail as the main artery.

Chatham Square

Today, Chatham Square is a largely forgotten corner of an ever-evolving metropolis; but the history of the Bowery begins here, at the foot of one of the most notorious yet culturally influential thoroughfares in the world. The old native lookout hill turned Dutch picnic ground turned freed slave cattle farm (which was eventually given the English name of Chatham Square in honor of William Pitt, Earl of Chatham) developed as a vital locale during the colonization of New York.

When King Charles II of England requested a permanent route be created between his new colonies, 250 miles of Native American trails, including the old Wickquasgeck Trail, were cleared and marked between Wall Street in Manhattan and Washington Street in Boston, Massachusetts. The first post rider left city hall on January 1, 1673, and took the treacherous, two-week journey on horseback through the hostile wilderness at the rate of about 18 miles per day. Though originally intended for military communiqué, official postal service was established on the Boston Post Road in 1691. Chatham Square housed the horse stables for the postal riders.

By the mid-1700s a stagecoach service was established that would carry passengers along the route as far as they wanted to go for a few cents per mile. Though pedestrian travel along this passage was nothing new for early colonists, until now, navigating the rough and foreign trails usually required the accompaniment of a local Indian guide. Over the next century, the road would be widened to allow wagons and three alternate routes to Boston laid, ranging from 225 to 270 miles long. As travel between colonies became easier,

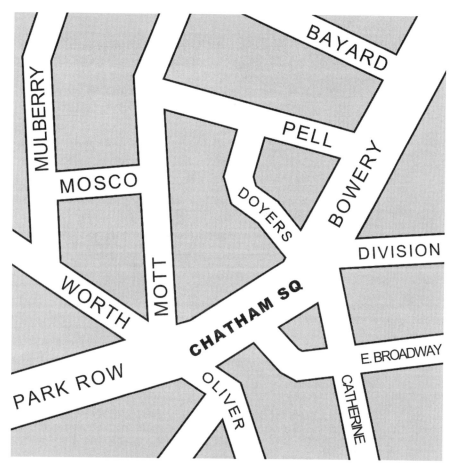

Map of Chatham Square. *Courtesy of Lower East Side History Project.*

the new Boston Post Road, or "King's Highway," as it was referred to, saw a steady increase in traffic, and entire communities would organically evolve along this route as businesses opened catering to the weary traveler. (Some of this early route would later become part of America's first highway system.)

Chatham Square was an important stop along the Boston Post Road. It offered the first depot for travelers entering the city (Harlem was roughly seven miles away), so a vital outdoor trading post and market evolved as local farmers would meet travelers here to sell and trade goods and livestock.

In 1749, Nicolas Bayard II, a major landowner and assistant alderman, made a cozy deal between prominent livestock butcher-farmers and the city to host a public slaughterhouse on his property, which covered the west side of the Bowery between roughly Chatham Square and Rivington Street. That

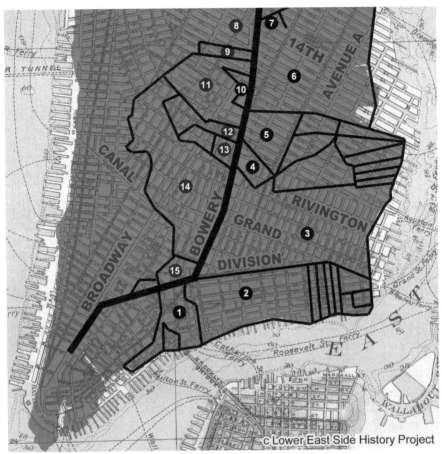

Major Bowery Landowners of the 18th Century

= Approximate estate boundaries
= Original outline of Manhattan Island

1 - Webber & Loockerman
2 - Rutger
3 - Delancey
4 - Van Courtland
5 - Minthorne
6 - Stuyvesant
7 - Anderson
8 - Bevoort

9 - "Sailor's Snug Harbor"
10 - Pero
11 - Herring
12 - Bleecker
13 - Tucker
14 - Bayard
15 - Kingston, Doyer, Delancey plots

Courtesy of Lower East Side History Project.

year, a law was passed that forbade any citizen from slaughtering any livestock whatsoever outside of this new facility, which was located on the site of today's southwest corner of Mulberry and Bayard Streets. At the time, it was the eastern bank of the collect pond.

On Bayard's property, just below today's Canal Street, sat an old tavern named the Half Way House (no. 46–48 Bowery), where proprietor Stephen Carpenter also operated a small cattle farm. Since Carpenter's farm adjoined the new slaughterhouse property to the west, the Half Way House became a center for drovers and butchers to negotiate deals or kill some time waiting for their turn to slaughter their livestock.

By the early 1750s, a Half Way House sign that hung above the door of the tavern was removed. It was replaced with a swinging wooden sign displaying a "ferocious" bull's head logo on either side, distinguishing it as a livestock farm. The property became known as "Bull's Head on Bowery Lane," and it would became one of the largest and most important livestock markets, or "Bull's Heads," in the Northeast. It served the entire Tri-State area, with reports of farmers from as far away as Ohio transporting entire herds to trade and sell at the Bowery's bull market.

The tavern became an unofficial headquarters for the local livestock trade; a place where drinking and socializing was a popular pastime, as was gambling (a favorite was a game called "crack loo"). Patrons could also bet on horse races along the Bowery Lane and highly publicized dog, bear, bull and cockfights that took place either inside or near the slaughterhouse. These were not men of low status; butchers, at the time, were some of the wealthiest and most politically connected businessmen in the city. The butchers and farmers, after all, fed the population.

An entire community sprang up around the property as many butchers purchased land as close to the slaughterhouse as possible. Mulberry Street for example, which bordered Bull's Head, became known as "Slaughterhouse Street" because of the rows of butchers who lined the block.

Nicolas Bayard II died in 1765, leaving the family estate to his son, Nicolas Bayard III, who in turn hired a reputable third-generation butcher named Richard Varian to run the operations of the slaughterhouse and, by 1773, the tavern. When the Revolutionary War began in 1775, Varian abandoned the market and joined the military to fight the British; however, he would be captured and imprisoned in Halifax. It would be several months after the end of the war before Varian was able to return home to the Bowery.

REVOLUTION

In the spring of 1776, to prepare for an invasion of the Brits, General George Washington and his army fortified strategic locations in Manhattan, Brooklyn and New Jersey. Every troop, civilian, servant and slave available in the city was recruited for the effort. Those who did not support the Revolution either fled or were arrested.

By the summer of 1776, the entire island of Manhattan was militarized with more than ten thousand Continental army troops and militiamen. The Bowery played a key role in maneuvering soldiers and supplies and ran through the army's largest encampment. Several Bowery landowners, like the Stuyvesants and Bayards, volunteered their estates and homes (perhaps begrudgingly); others, like British Loyalist James DeLancey, gave up their property when they fled to England.

As the only major road into the city, the Bowery was fitted with a multitude of blockades, check points and heavy weapons. Five brigades were assigned to the Lower East Side area, which was canvassed with

A 1776 map of Lower Manhattan. The Bowery is marked as "Road to King's Bridge where the Rebels mean to make a Stand." *Boston Public Library Digital Map Collection.*

thousands and thousands of tents, wagons, barricades, supply shacks, ammo dumps, horses and military personnel. Its landscape was literally torn apart—trees, fences and old wooden structures were sacrificed for firewood and blockades, and soldiers rifled through houses and stomped through farms and gardens. Several strategic batteries were engineered in the neighborhood, connected by a network of deep trenches with no regard for property lines, located at Broome and Pitt Streets (eight cannons), Grand and Norfolk (eight cannons), Grand and Eldridge (eight cannons), Catherine and Cherry (two cannons), Clinton and Montgomery (six cannons) and Broome and Forsyth.

To the west of the Bowery, just north of the old Kalck-Hook (now simply referred to as the "Collect Pond"), a fort was built atop the mighty elevation on the Bayard estate that once sheltered the people of Werpoes. "Bayard's Mount" was turned into Bayard's Hill Redoubt, better known as "Bunker Hill"—a heptagonal fortress with six mortars, twelve cannons and a 360-degree view of Lower Manhattan. Notable Captain Nathan Hale was stationed at Bunker Hill, where he kept a diary describing an anxious infantry waiting for battle: "For about six or eight days the enemy have been expected hourly, whenever the wind and tide least favored...The place and manner of attack time must determine. The event we leave to Heaven."

On June 28, 1776, a Continental army soldier assigned to George Washington's personal security detail was hanged in a field at Bowery and Grand Street. Thomas Hickey was convicted of being a counterfeiter; however, history suggests that he may have been involved in a wider conspiracy to assassinate Washington. Known as the "Hickey Plot," the facts have polarized historians and researchers for over two hundred years. Reports claim that twenty thousand people, including Alexander Hamilton, turned out to witness the hanging—because Washington ordered the entire city present.

In August 1776, the seventeen-thousand-strong British allies finally made their move and engaged the Continental army in Long Island (Brooklyn). Washington's troops were overwhelmed and forced to retreat, giving up Long Island and eventually Manhattan Island. The occupying force simply seized the forts and batteries created by Washington's army and took up arms for the next seven years.

The Treaty of Paris, which ended the war, was signed on September 3, 1783. On the morning of November 25, the British military began to evacuate the city via the Bowery, marching south toward the docks at Whitehall Street. General Knox and his troops followed behind them, stopping at the present site of Cooper Union (Bowery and Astor Place) for two hours while the British orchestrated their procession. The entire city was reclaimed by 3:00 p.m.

Later that day, General George Washington met up with Knox, the troops and other luminaries at the Bull's Head Tavern before their celebrated victory march through Chatham Square into the city. Though Bull's Head owner Richard Varian was not present, his wife and family of eighteen reclaimed the property as the British evacuated and opened it in time for the historic event.

In 1789, America's first presidential inaugural ball was held for Washington at the old DeLancey house on the Bowery at Canal Street, just a short stroll from his home at 1 Cherry Street.

By the end of the war, the old Bull's Head public slaughterhouse was in severe disrepair after being abandoned for nearly a decade. The industry had changed dramatically since old laws prohibiting butchers to slaughter livestock outside of the Bull's Head didn't apply during the war; this saved farmers a lot of time and money. Most butchers were resistant to return to the former system, and subsequently, the slaughterhouse was closed; the entire industry moved over to Corlear's Hook on the East River. The cattle farm and tavern remained, however, and would get a new landlord by 1787, a man named Heinrich (Henry) Astor.

UTOPIA

In the years immediately following the war, New York City took a giant leap toward becoming the global center of commerce and culture we know today as fortune-seekers from around the globe poured into the city to stake a claim in the capital of the new America. One of the most notable was Heinrich Astor (1754–1833), the first of his clan to settle in the United States. Just twenty-two years old at the time, the former Waldorf peasant would plant the seeds of one of America's wealthiest dynasties right here on the Bowery.

Astor arrived in America during the Revolution at twenty-two years old as a sutler (a citizen who sells provisions to the military) with the Hessian army, which was hired out by the British to support their effort in the war. He stepped on Manhattan soil for the first time as the British-Hessian allies entered the city after the Battle of Brooklyn in August 1776. Here, Astor established himself as a butcher—a trade his father had taught him back in Europe—and he secured a minor contract to supply beef and produce to English troops and Loyalist regiments.

After the war ended, Astor remained in New York City, became a citizen, Anglicized his first name to "Henry," married and opened a butcher stall at the Old Oswego Market on Broadway. By 1789, he had moved to a booth at the entrance of the Fly Market on Maiden Lane. In May 1790, his competitors complained that Astor was blocking the entrance to the market and essentially pirating all of the customers. A petition to have Astor's booth relocated was successful, and his stall was moved to the lower market, at the foot of the East River.

Astor's business "savvy" made him one of the most successful butchers in the city by the time he became a Bowery property owner in the 1780s. According to one-time Bull's Head Market owner Daniel Drew, as the city's butchers gathered at the tavern to wait for a herd to enter the city, young Henry Astor would slip out the back door and ride up the Bowery to cut off the drover in order to select the prime livestock before any other butchers had a chance.

Henry wrote many letters back to Europe, excited about the potential of success in the new country, which inspired his younger brother Johann's move to New York City in 1784. Though business was not great in the years immediately following the Revolution (not many people remained in the city), with Henry's connections, Johann Jacob Astor (July 17, 1763–March 29, 1848) began a series of odd jobs along the docks where he had developed relationships with sea-bound fur traders. Johann learned the trade inside and out and made a fortune in the importing/exporting business, while Henry's butcher business expanded as the population grew. The brothers reinvested their money in the post-Revolution land grab of Manhattan Island, and Johann became the first multimillionaire in America. The Astor family would remain, for the next two hundred years, one of the wealthiest and most influential dynasties in this city.

Men like the Astors helped New York City go from colonial backwater to world-renowned cosmopolitan city and center of American commerce in a matter of decades. Chatham Square grew into a cluster of upscale shops and services and attracted some of the city's wealthiest population. Fashionable families bought up properties in proximity to the Post Road, and an upscale community evolved. There was no longer a desire to have a fetid, unsightly cattle farm in the middle of an upper-class neighborhood, so Henry Astor's neighbors bought him out by 1820.

The cattle farm moved to a rural area at Twenty-fourth Street and Third Avenue. Many sources say the tavern lasted until 1825, when it was torn down to make way for a massive new theater (though, according to an 1838 *Niles National Register*, the theater was built adjacent to the old tavern and the original structure was destroyed along with the theater in a fire).

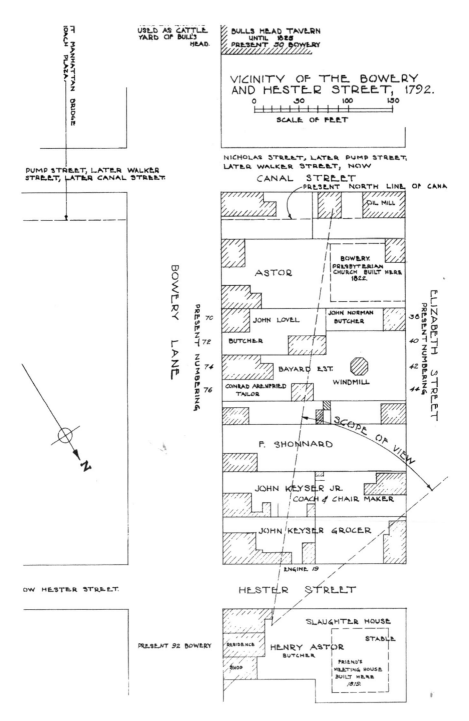

A 1792 map of the Bowery at Canal Street. *From* Old Bowery Days: The Chronicles of a Famous Street, *by Alvin Fay Harlow, 1931.*

The Edward Mooney House at 18 Bowery today. *Courtesy of Shirley Dluginski.*

The Bull's Head on the Bowery was such a popular destination for so long that it made its way into the American vernacular in a phrase that was common until the end of the nineteenth century: "Don't tell so and so, or it will be known before night from Bull's Head to the Battery," or, "I can be back in the time it takes to get from the Bull's Head to the Battery."

The only surviving American Revolution–era row house on Manhattan Island, the Edward Mooney House, stands at the southwest corner of Bowery and Pell Street. It was built for prominent butcher and wholesaler Edward Mooney sometime between 1785 and 1789 and designated a National Historic Landmark in 1965. This building is a prime example of early Federal-era construction and the type of residencies occupied by the upper classes of eighteenth-century New York.

When the City of New York officially confiscated James DeLancey's farm after the war, it divided the land up and sold individual lots in a forfeiture sale. Mooney purchased this property, which included three and a half lots, in September 1784 and built a handsome two-story structure soon after. In 1807, another floor was added, but few alterations were made to this building until it was fully restored in 1971.

One of New York's earliest professional theatres, the Park, opened on Chatham Square in January 1798. Over the next couple of decades,

Chatham Square today, with Confucius Plaza hovering in the background. *Courtesy of Shirley Dluginski.*

several prestigious entertainment venues, like the Chatham and New-York Theatres, followed, and the Bowery emerged as the epicenter of high society in the new metropolis.

Real estate speculator Jacob Astor leased out land on the Bowery between Astor Place and Bond Street in 1805 to a Frenchman named Delacroix, who opened the opulent Vauxhall Gardens. It was a beautiful, finely manicured public space lined with colorful flower beds, marble statues, park benches and a small outdoor stage that offered choral performances and special events, attracting the city's elite. Luxurious town houses and mansions were constructed around the park, and some of the most prominent families in the country flocked to the new neighborhood. As Astor planned, the Bowery and Bond Street area would become the most fashionable address in America by the 1820s.

In 1811, the street grid we know today was implemented above Houston Street, and in 1812 a new city hall opened at its present location between Broadway and Park Row (originally Chatham Street). Most remaining geographical features of Mannahatta, E-hen-da-wi-kih-tit (or whatever it was actually called) were dredged, dug, leveled, filled in or drained to make way for the new street grid. Bunker Hill became landfill for the Collect Pond. The waterfront was expanded to accommodate growing commerce. Old fields and farms were sliced into ordered blocks. New York City was preparing for an economic boom. The population of New York City in 1790 was approximately 49,401, but by 1830 it swelled to 242,278.

Melting Pot

By the 1830s, Chatham Square and the Bowery (its "Lane" suffix dropped in 1808) had become a much less important thoroughfare with the development of nearby Broadway and other avenues. The local population was less concentrated as neighborhoods sprang up throughout the island above Fourteenth Street and residents migrated north. The Bowery had emerged from this transition a decidedly commercial district.

An 1839 *Ladies Companion and Literary Expositor* article claims that Chatham Square shops were still "more brilliant at night than those in Broadway, the side-walks spacious and clean, and, altogether, affording one of the most interesting promenades of an evening (especially Saturday) to be found in Gotham." However, like much of the neighborhood, the old native lookout turned picnic ground turned...you get the idea...was about to undergo yet another change, as waves of working-class Irish, German and other immigrants poured into the local wards, drastically altering the city's ordered future imagined by city planners and real estate tycoons.

The German population concentrated in the Tenth and Seventeenth Wards, to the east of the Upper Bowery—a district that became known as Kleindeutschland ("Little Germany") because it contained the third-largest population of Germans in the world at the time. Many escaped a failed revolution and transferred their radical spirit to the New World, becoming some of the earliest labor and community organizers in the city. Many of these immigrants were educated; craftsmen, artisans, musicians, publishers, lawyers, doctors and other professionals prepared for transition to a burgeoning city—unlike many of their Irish contemporaries who arrived unskilled in urban labor.

The Irish settled in the Sixth, Fourth and Seventh Wards along the Lower Bowery for several reasons. Primarily, many were shipbuilders and seamen, and a large portion of the shipping industry at the time was located in the Fourth and Seventh Wards. And over in the Sixth, an early century attempt to fill in the old Collect Pond and build a community over it failed when the houses sunk back into the earth, leaving it the most undesirable location in

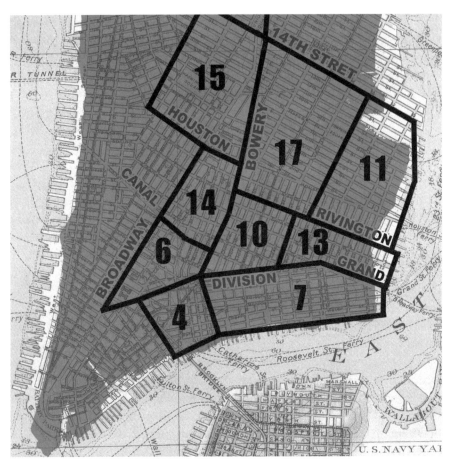

19th Century Ward Boundaries

Courtesy of Lower East Side History Project.

the city (so basically, no one else wanted to live there). A small black, working-class and working-poor community already existed in these wards by the time the Irish arrived in large numbers. Many "respectable" families in the district moved elsewhere and discovered the value of renting out their former homes as cheap lodging houses.

Though on opposite sides of the social spectrum, both immigrant groups would thrive in the foreign land and have an enduring effect on the future of New York City. By the end of the century, the German and Irish made up a majority of the city administration and political landscape; however, it was not an easy transition. Accounts of Chatham Square/Lower Bowery by the late 1840s describe a rough-and-tumble district comprising a streetscape that was more utilitarian than aesthetic. Rows of small, uneven and unkempt stores, lodging houses and saloons littered the thoroughfare, and Chatham Square had become a marketplace for second-hand goods. Vendors and auctioneers would pimp their merchandise—used furniture, jewelry, silverware, hardware, clothing—from seven- by nine-foot "boxes" lined along the sidewalks. "Street criers" could be heard at every step, "Twent'-five for them pants..." Pawnshops were abundant, identified by three gilt balls that adorned the entranceway. Inside, pawnbrokers would wheel and deal in secrecy behind large boxes of merchandise that faced away from the curtained front door.

Chatham Square had become synonymous with "tough" and "rugged." In a September 1841 boxing match where notable bare-knuckle pugilist Tom Hyer was getting the better of Yankee Sullivan trainer "Country McClusky," Country's corner man tried to rally the boxer between rounds by saying, "Give 'em one of those Chatham Square fellows!" Unfortunately for Country McClusky, it didn't work. He gave up to Hyer after the 101st round (and over three hours of getting socked in the face by a champion).

A May 17, 1858 *New York Times* article states, "That portion of the Sixth Ward side of the Bowery extending from Chatham Square to Canal Street, is generally known as the rowdies' retreat. Almost every doorstep is crowded with 'fancy' and 'fighting men,' who delight in exhibiting themselves to the passers in a manner not at all agreeable to decent folk."

By the time of the Civil War, once proud professional establishments along the Lower Bowery had long since moved out, sold out or adjusted to the working-class immigrant masses, working poor, transients and down-on-their-luck opportunists who now made up their patronage. The avenue devolved into a mecca for saloons, gambling parlors, opium dens, flophouses, brothels, pawnshops, second-hand stores and low-brow entertainment venues featuring black-face minstrelsy, burlesque and cabarets.

By this time, gangsterism and politics were completely married through alliances between organizations like Tammany Hall and infamous gangs such as the Irish Dead Rabbits and Nativist Bowery Boys—a story well told by now. Organized gangs and corrupt officials united to make sure the underground economy ran smooth by headquartering out of Bowery social clubs and keeping a close eye on the action.

Depiction of Bowery b'hoy and Bowery girl. *From* The Illustrated Annuals of Phrenology and Physiognomy, *1869.*

The Upper Bowery was able to hold on to some respectability with institutions like Cooper Union, while upper-middle-class Germans made their mark with their own theaters, beer halls, social clubs, union halls, ballrooms, banks and hotels; however, the Upper Bowery's elegance would also deteriorate in the shadows of the elevated railroad, which was erected in 1878.

Introduction

Ward No.	1800	1820	1850	1880	1910
4	54,127	83,793	181,463	163,871	166,533
6	83,686	85,178	158,067	129,254	125,888
7	48,773	41,207	103,572	158,625	323,498
10		107,508	140,776	287,118	401,135
11			128,464	201,917	400,860
13			165,848	221,927	379,561
14			158.093	189,308	240,119
17			96,587	231,364	380,319
Other wards:					
1	10,473	29,297	47,888	43,488	23,867
2	43,512	69,171	56,042	13,541	7,857
3	40,464	57,732	64,973	22,475	12,016
5	36,140	49,071	89,624	62,598	22,384

Population per square mile. *Courtesy of Lower East Side History Project, based on data from the U.S. Census Bureau and demographia.com.*

The neighborhood faced a new set of challenges when waves of predominantly Eastern and Southern European immigrants began to flood the city in the 1870s, resulting in the Lower East Side becoming one of the most densely populated two square miles on the face of the earth by the end of the century. As a general rule, Southern Europeans (Italians, Sicilians) settled to the west of the Bowery, eventually displacing most of the Irish population. Eastern Europeans (Jews, Poles, etc.) settled to the east of the Bowery, eventually displacing much of the German population. America's great "melting pot" was boiling over, and the Bowery once again found itself cradling a political, social and cultural powder keg.

Like the immigrants before them, the new arrivals would have a profound effect on the future of the city (and country) by contributing to great advances in education, labor and women's rights, social service, publishing, politics and arts and entertainment, to name a very few—and the Bowery was a petri dish of experimentation where these influences were incubated.

However, by the 1890s, the Bowery was ripe for wanton corruption (perfected over decades) and had openly become one of the greatest vice districts in America. It was the original "city that never sleeps," the Times Square of its day, an epicenter of nefarious recreation and amusement in the heart of one of the poorest neighborhoods in the world. The Bowery's immigrant theater, gambling parlors, brothels, saloons, curiosity museums, sideshows and cheap amusements attracted the masses and lined the pockets of thoroughly corrupt city officials.

As criminal as it all sounds (and was), the Bowery was progressive for its time and has always seemed to stay one step ahead of the cultural curve. Cercle Hermaphroditos, Golden Rule Pleasure Club, the Palm, Manilla Hall, Black Rabbit, Little Buck's and, most notably, Columbia Hall at 392 Bowery (better known as Paresis Hall) were just a few of the openly gay clubs, saloons, bathhouses and theaters in the district by 1892. Though perhaps the earliest (certainly the most prominent) gay districts in America, these establishments attracted revelers of every type. It became part of the "Bowery experience" to mingle with "fairies" and "hermaphrodites." For gay men (and some women), it was a rare opportunity in the nineteenth century to interact socially without much discrimination, other than the occasional drunk sailor; for tourists and partygoers, it was just another curious attraction. Either way, the powers that be sheltered the community and allowed it to thrive.

A push by local merchants to change the name of the Bowery at the turn of the century failed when a city alderman argued, "Where will the soldiers and sailors go if we change the name of the Bowery? They will get lost looking all round New York on their days off ship, and the efficiency of the army and navy will be impaired. Change the flag of the country, but don't change the name of the Bowery."

Several attempts to change the name of the Bowery over the next century (to disassociate the district from its marginal past) have failed, though the community was successful in renaming a portion of the Bowery from East Eighth Street to East Fourth Street in the 1880s, when the Cooper Square address was introduced.

Skid Row

The opening of the Williamsburg Bridge (1903), New York City subway system (1908) and Manhattan Bridge (1912) helped alleviate much of the overcrowding on the Lower East Side by the early twentieth century as businesses and entire communities relocated to Brooklyn and other neighborhoods. Both bridges opened up onto the Bowery (at Canal and Delancey Streets); as a result, an unprecedented volume of vehicle and pedestrian traffic further cemented the Bowery's commercial district future.

The Golden Age of the Bowery was fading. By the 1920s and '30s, nearly all of the union halls, theaters and museums were long gone, replaced by manufacturers, warehouses and lodging houses. Population relocation, an economic depression and a concerted local and federal effort to eradicate vice and corruption took their toll on the old entertainment district. All that remained were a few small businesses, greasy spoon diners, shelters and flophouses.

At the height of the Great Depression, tens of thousands of men and women sought refuge daily on the Bowery at one of its many spirituality-based missions. The Bowery earned its "Skid Row" moniker and reputation as a haven for the homeless and destitute during this time period; the thoroughfare would never really shake this association.

Rebirth

In the years following World War II, a large number of students, musicians and artists moved into the industrial, working-class, immigrant neighborhood, attracted by cheap commercial rents and large, empty spaces (former theaters, hotels and warehouses). Rather than shun the Bowery's marginal past, many embraced it; the Bowery fed, sheltered and inspired them, visible in the pioneering art coming out of the era, such as the beatniks, abstract expressionism, Bebop and experimental theater.

The Bowery was where Rothko, shrouded by a shabby hat and coat, could withdraw from his elite pedigree (famously indistinguishable from the drunks and hobos); where Kerouac would share greasy soup, strong coffee and life stories with "respectable bums"; and where "Bird" rubbed elbows with Slavic barflies, when he wasn't busy changing the future of jazz. These new arrivals invigorated the Bowery, and a resurgence of arts and culture emerged after lying dormant for several decades.

In 1957, the landmark Third Avenue elevated train was closed and the tracks removed. Many attribute the beginning of gentrification of the Lower East Side to this event, as the symbolic border between the East Side and Greenwich Village had been erased.

A 1960 *New York Times* headline announced, "The Village Spills Across 3rd Avenue," and reported how the neighborhood east of the Bowery was already being referred to as "Village East" or "East Village." Landlords, real estate professionals and small businesses began to capitalize on the new name, and by the 1980s, the term "East Village" had became commonly accepted.

On the Lower Bowery, a restaurant and lighting wholesaler district emerged, and by the 1960s, Chinatown and its retailers—for nearly a century relegated to the Chatham Square area—swelled north toward Delancey Street.

Today, extensive development is underway on the Bowery. Astor's old stomping ground is returning to the aristocratic roots abandoned almost two hundred years ago. High-rise hotels, four-star restaurants, stylish condos and large-scale nightclubs share the streetscape with what is remaining of the artists, family-operated small businesses and 150-year-old landmarks.

CHINATOWN

The seeds of what would become the largest population of Chinese people outside of Asia were sown in the mid-nineteenth century, when a merchant named Ah Ken arrived in 1858 and settled on Mott Street. Ah Ken opened a cigar store on Park Row, became very successful and attracted other Chinese merchants to the neighborhood—most notably Wah Kee, a Cantonese man who arrived in New York City by way of San Francisco and opened an Asian goods store at 13 Pell Street, near the corner of Doyers, in 1866.

By the late 1860s, there were perhaps only dozens of Chinese residents in New York City, but a violent backlash against foreign workers in the California gold rush sent many Chinese fleeing to more tolerant cities in the East. Others lost their jobs after completing immense railroad projects out west, forcing them to look for work in large cities like New York, while many others were lured to the city by employers to work in local cigar factories, as launderers or on the farms of Long Island. The Chinese Exclusion Act of 1882 prevented the population from growing significantly until the mid-twentieth century, so for the first few decades of its existence, Chinatown was a small, isolated and virtually autonomous neighborhood centered on Doyers, Mott and Pell Streets.

The concerns of local Chinese residents were essentially neglected by the city administration, so community leaders rallied for the formation of an organization that represented their interests. As a result, the Chinese Charitable and Benevolent Association of the City of New York was organized in 1883 and incorporated in 1890. Today, the CCBA is known as Chinese Consolidated Benevolent Association and is the oldest organization in Chinatown.

Above: A Chinese band, circa 1880. *From* New York's Chinatown: An Historical Presentation of Its People and Places, *by Louis Joseph Beck.*

Right: Chinatown illustrations. *From* The American Metropolis, *1879*.

Chinese migrants settled in small colonies throughout the Five Boroughs and New Jersey, but Doyers Street evolved into the epicenter of the community's commercial and social activity by the end of the nineteenth century. Social clubs, ethnic markets and labor and civic associations were headquartered here, and in March 1893, New York City's first professional Chinese Theater opened at 5–7 Doyers. It was only the second public theater in the city dedicated to Chinese performances, the first being a small storefront at 19 Bowery. Because of its convenient location at the foot of the Chatham Square elevated train station, the new "Chinatown" attracted not only Chinese but also shoppers, sightseers and the purely curious from all over the Tri-State area.

The establishment of a Chinese Consulate in 1878 and a visit from Viceroy Li Hung-Chang on a goodwill mission in 1896 helped slightly soften America's sentiment toward the Chinese by the end of the century. Though Chinese were still not allowed to become U.S. citizens, the American public developed a curious attraction with the Orient. Many merchants in Chinatown welcomed the economic potential and began catering to western patrons.

The Chinese Exclusion Act was nullified in 1943, which allowed a small number of immigrants to trickle in from China. But in 1965, all quotas were lifted, leading to massive waves of Chinese from all over Asia pouring into New York City. By the 1970s, Chinatown had expanded considerably, covering roughly two square miles to either side of Lower Bowery between Chatham Square and Canal Street.

In December 1975, a massive, forty-four-story, mixed-use housing, commercial and community complex named Confucius Plaza opened on the Bowery at the foot of the Manhattan Bridge. It was the first major publicly funded housing project built for Chinese use in the city and includes 764 apartments, a day-care center, a school, retail and commercial space and a community center.

The $45 million development got the green light from the city in October 1972, and ground was broken one year later. Five acres of land were cleared, including the popular Chinese Garden park near the corner of Canal and Bowery and several century-old structures. The new superstructure was intended to alleviate some of the overcrowding in the neighborhood.

Though affordable housing and other amenities were welcomed by most of the community, a backlash began when the management company refused to hire Asian workers on the construction site. Many historians point to the ensuing community battle as a turning point in discrimination against Chinese American workers in New York City.

Introduction

The civil rights organization Asian Americans for Equality (originally Asian Americans for Equal Employment) was founded in 1974 in response to discrimination at the Confucius Plaza site. The AAFE and others requested several meetings with both the developer and city agencies, but appeals went unanswered. Direct action began in the spring of 1974, when the AAFE organized marches on the construction site. On May 16, forty-eight protesters were arrested, which only united the community further.

Developers gave in within six months, and Chinese workers were hired. It was a major victory for the people of Chinatown and the first time the community organized on such a scale. From this incident, the Chinese American community emerged as a formidable political force in this city.

Chinatown today is a thriving, continuously sprawling district and one of the last ethnic enclaves in New York City.

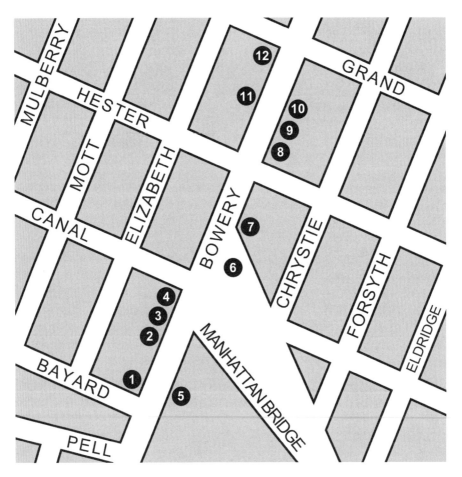

Addresses discussed in this chapter. *Courtesy of Lower East Side History Project.*

Chapter 2

Bayard Street to Grand Street

30–36 BOWERY

In 1826, the grand North American Hotel was built on this corner of Bowery and Bayard Street, replacing a small grocery store that was destroyed by a fire. The hotel fronted four lots along the Bowery and wrapped around the corner along Bayard, forming the shape of an L. In the basement was a supper club, which quickly became a hot spot for the bustling after-theater crowd of the 1830s and '40s. The most celebrated actors, circus performers and athletes of the era frequented the hotel, and many bare-knuckle boxing contests were arranged here, including an 1849 fight between noted pugilist Mat Gooderson and champion Tom Hyer (who also managed the hotel bar and ran a gambling enterprise at 36 Bowery for over a decade).

According to William Ellis Horton's *Driftwood of the Stage*, the Virginia Minstrels, America's first professional minstrel group, got their big break in the billiard room of the hotel in 1843, when owner Jonas Bartlett gave them a chance to entertain the well-connected audience. The Minstrels had been in New York performing short skits at obscure circuses and living at the hotel when this impromptu performance landed them a headlining gig at the Bowery Amphitheater.

By 1855, the hotel had fallen into the hands of proprietor Daniel Moss, who redesigned the interior and reopened it as the Branch Hotel. The property adjoining the hotel to the west (corner of Bayard and Elizabeth Streets) was occupied by the Butts & Shaw Stables, headquarters of the infamous "Stable

Gang," a cabal of prominent politicos and businessmen who helped guide "Boss" William M. Tweed's scandalous political career. Daniel Moss recalls preparing meals like fresh soft-shell crabs from City Island, which they would "devour with copious draughts of wine," in the hotel kitchen for the group's secret stable meetings.

According to Moss, the congressmen, aldermen, judges and businessmen of the Stable Gang would divide their time between the hotel and the stables. In an 1891 interview, the former hotel owner reflected, "All the political disorder with which the city seemed to be persistently possessed was quickly reflected in these corners."

It was at this corner of Bowery and Bayard Street that the first battle in the bloody three-day war between the Dead Rabbits and Bowery Boys took place in 1857. The city was quite literally polarized by the summer of '57 as Mayor Fernando Wood refused the State Supreme Court's orders to resign from office on charges of corruption. In support of Mayor Wood, much of his administration also refused to step down, including the municipal police force. During this time, long-running tensions boiled over, and battle lines were decidedly drawn between the ethnic and conservative enclaves of Lower Manhattan, causing several violent skirmishes.

On July 2, 1857, after months of disorder, Wood finally stepped aside, and his police disbanded. The ex-mayor's supporters in the Five Points were greatly disappointed and became enraged when, the next day, word got out that the new Metropolitan Police Department had hired no Irishmen. Rumors of conspiracies spread throughout the Sixth Ward, only fueling the fire, and shortly after midnight on July 4, the Dead Rabbits and other Five Point gangs organized en masse in Chatham Square looking to dispose of any new policemen in their district.

The mob attacked several officers as they moved north toward 40 Bowery, the headquarters of the Bowery Boys, which was adjacent to the Branch Hotel. After pummeling no. 40 Bowery (and several men) with sticks and paving stones, the rioters turned their attention to the Branch Hotel. Patrons of the hotel held the mob at bay until an army of Bowery Boys and Atlantic Guards arrived to drive the mob away. "In less than five minutes over 300 had collected," claimed a witness. The Rabbits retreated, only to regroup for a larger confrontation later that day, which would last throughout the weekend and result in hundreds of casualties.

The Branch Hotel survived and was remodeled as the New England Hotel by 1864. On January 13 of that year, a fever-struck guest of the hotel fell, hit his head against a wash bin and died three days later from his injury. The

Dead Rabbits and Bowery Boys clash in 1857. *Courtesy of Library of Congress.*

man's name was Stephen Foster, a thirty-seven-year-old songwriter who would posthumously become known as the "Father of American Music."

Stephen Collins Foster was born on the fiftieth anniversary of our nation's birthday, July 4, 1826, in Lawrenceville, Pennsylvania, and signed his first contract in December 1844 with G. Willig of Philadelphia, who published his song, "Open Thy Lattice Love." Foster's first venture was not successful, but three years later his song "Oh Susanna" would become a national sensation, and a string of hits were to follow, which included "Camptown Races," "Jeannie with the Light Brown Hair" and "Old Folks Home" (known to many as "Swanee River").

As successful as he was, Foster was paid very little for his craft. There was no music business at the time, no royalties or merchandising, no copyright protection. He was paid a flat fee by a music publisher for each song, and this practice sometimes earned him no more than fifty bucks. Foster's songwriting style fell out of fashion by the Civil War, and he wound up despondent and broke on the Bowery, where he died with thirty-eight cents in his pocket and a note that simply read, "Dear friends and gentle hearts."

In 1880, Reverend Albert Gleason Ruliffson, his wife and a small group of supporters rented a room at 36 Bowery that they adapted into a gospel mission. The Bowery Mission, as it would come to be known, stayed at this location for only about a decade but went on to serve Manhattan's homeless and working poor for the next 130 years, over 100 of which were at 227 Bowery, where it continues to operate today.

In 1891, 34 and 36 Bowery were purchased by the Third Avenue Rail Company to make way for an elevated train cable and power station, thus ending the hotel's sixty-five-year run of extraordinary history.

Today, the address hosts a large mixed-use apartment complex and office space.

37–39 BOWERY

This is the site of one of the earliest permanent wildlife menageries in the United States, called the Zoological Institute. Built in 1833, the institute offered the United States its first chance to examine many exotic animals from around the world up close and personal.

It was a grand structure that stretched all the way to Christie Street, covering four city lots. For only fifty cents (half price for children), visitors would be able to examine a wide variety of species in the immense indoor gallery—bears, tigers, monkeys, hyenas, snakes, vultures, zebras—all kept in individual cells along the sides of a lengthy hall. At the far end of the gallery was a rhinoceros, flanked by elephants and lions, as part of the "African Glen" exhibit (which was on loan from the Coliseum in London).

Each exhibit offered beautiful displays and panoramas individualized for each animal's natural habitat. The floors of the exhibits had a slight incline leading to a drainage system that ran the length of the hall; this helped keep the cages clean and eliminate much of the odor. The cages were numbered and corresponded to a guidebook visitors were given that included information about the animals. The main gallery was illuminated during the day by several skylights on the ceiling and at night by three stately gas-lit chandeliers. Above the caged animals was an orchestra promenade and theater-like seating for special events, like lion taming, circus performances and equestrian shows, which took place at the center of the hall.

In 1835, the building was modified with a stage and renamed the Bowery Amphitheater. Some sources say half the building was still dedicated to a menagerie, though the new theater began offering a variety of entertainment options.

P.T. Barnum's flair for words landed him a job in 1841 as an ad writer at the Bowery Amphitheater, where, according to an autobiography, he made a paltry four dollars a week. (His next gig made him a fortune, when he opened Barnum's American Museum on Broadway later that year.)

Though the venue continued to offer circus performances and equestrian shows, programming changed by the mid-1840s as minstrelsy became the norm. One of its premier acts, the Virginia Minstrels, performed the first headlining, full-length group minstrel show in the United States at the Bowery Amphitheater in 1843, inspiring a slew of copycats.

By 1854, 37–39 Bowery hosted the New York Stadt Theater, a well-respected venue for German plays and operas. The Stadt was led by a succession of highly regarded managers, including Adolph Neuendorff, who directed the theater between 1863 and 1867 before going on to lead the New York Philharmonic.

The New York Stadt Theater lasted at this location until 1864 before moving to 45 Bowery for the next eight years. By 1880, the name had been changed to the Windsor Theater, and by 1885, 37 Bowery appears to have had a roller rink on its premises called Windsor Roller Skating Rink.

In December 1897, the Peniel Mission moved into 39 Bowery under the direction of A.W. Dennet, who named it the "Peniel Josephine Mission" in honor of his wife. The Peniel Missionary Society was founded by Holiness Movement pioneer Theodore Pollock Ferguson and his wife, Manie, in Los Angeles in 1886. A large donation allowed the mission to expand to a couple of dozen cities by 1904, including this location, the first Peniel Mission on the East Coast.

On November 30, 1900, A.W. Dennet re-imagined his enterprise and re-launched the mission as the Ragged Church, which was said to be modeled after a London church of the same name. About 450 men gathered for the opening services, attracted by the free buns and tolerant dress code.

Not everyone was impressed. A *New York City Mission Monthly* article said, "Our own past experience in the Bowery enables us to predict crowded attendance so long as the crullers and rolls hold out." Perhaps they were right; the Ragged Church closed within two years.

This address is now part of the Confucius Plaza complex.

46–48 BOWERY

In 1827, the *New York Literary Gazette* announced the opening of a new theater on the site of the old Bull's Head cattle market: "A *new theatre* will be erected in the course on the present year of the site of the old Bull's head, and, if we may trust to sage prognostication it will prove a dangerous rival to our present establishments."

The New-York Theatre, Bowery was the official name, and it would be only the third such venue in the city (as well as the largest, and first gas-lit, in the country). Built to satisfy the local aristocratic community, its three thousand seats, stately neoclassical, Greek temple–like design and lavish interior were said to rival any playhouse in London or Paris. Its main competition was the renowned Park Theatre just below Chatham Square, considered the crux of high culture at the time—but it did not posses the New-York Theatre's size and aesthetic beauty.

As grand as it was, a new theater in Manhattan was not welcomed by everyone. Much of the conservative population was not adjusting well to the new cosmopolitan status of New York City and the hedonistic culture it bred. An 1826 *Magazine of the Reformed Dutch Church* article warned: "A theatre in this city was opened for the season on the Monday evening of last week. We do not mention this fact to give *information*;—we mention it to excite Christians to pray against the wide-spreading pestilence; to exhort Christian parents to keep their children from the vortex of destruction."

The *Christian Spectator* commented: "The influence of the theater is bad, and only bad," along with several more paragraphs of colorful passages like, "The theater cannot be reformed. We should just as soon think of reforming the devil himself."

However, it wasn't theatrics per se that had conservatives up in arms, though they did complain of productions that were lowbrow, amoral and obscene. It was the alcohol, prostitution and gambling that went hand in hand with a night on the town in the 1820s and '30s that really bothered them. For example, it was common practice for theaters to hire prostitutes from nearby Five Points to work the upper tiers of the auditorium, and liquor was served by waitresses of questionable morals who wore dresses that revealed their ankles.

The New-York Theatre, Bowery opened on October 22, 1826, under the management of Charles A. Gilfert with the play called *The Road to Ruin*. It followed up with equally solid productions, like *Othello*, starring homegrown hero Edwin Forrest (whom Gilfert tempted away from the Park with a fifty-dollar-a-week salary).

The new theater would steal some of the Park's thunder for a few years, but management soon found it difficult to fill three thousand seats regularly and meet the financial demands of the actors. So Gilfert decided to experiment with less refined programming in an attempt to broaden the theater's appeal beyond the upper classes.

An early theater playbill advertised itself as a "Great Novelty and Combination of Attraction," promoting such offerings as *The Black Schooner*,

An 1841 engraving of Thomas Hamblin as "Il Jattattore; or, the Evil Eye." *Original source: Gallery of Rascalities and Notorieties—No. 8.*

which promised "Piracy! Mutiny! & Murder!" and two-and-a-half-year-old "infant phenomenon" Le Petit Andreas in *Cupid & Zephyr*.

In February 1827, French dancer Madame Francisque Hutin performed the first solo ballet in America called *La Bergere Coquette* at the New-York Theatre—and also broke moral barriers as she performed in an outfit that exposed her knees. Needless to say, the resulting controversy only fueled more interest, and theatergoers were hooked.

In May 1828, a fire broke out in a stable on Bayard Street and rapidly spread north along the Bowery toward Canal Street, destroying almost every structure in its path, including the new theater. The venue was rebuilt within months, but as luck would have it, the venue was again destroyed by fire in 1836, 1838, 1845, 1923 and 1929. The 1838 fire caused one fatality on an adjoining property and a ruckus at the Zoological Institute across the street.

Charles Gilfert passed away in 1829, and the managerial duties of the theater were soon after placed in the hands of Thomas Sowerby Hamblin, a popular English-born actor who had gained much respect on the New York City stage. However, under Hamblin's leadership, any remaining aristocratic supporters soon returned to the Park.

By the 1830s, while the Park and other theaters continued to infuse European influence into New York City performing arts, the New-York Theatre, Bowery—now simply known as the Bowery Theater—would hire only American performers and playwrights. Hamblin took advantage of the overwhelming popularity of sensational and patriotic-themed entertainment among the working classes emerging in the district. The new Bowery Theater was welcomed with tremendous success and adopted by the plebeian residents of the Fourth and Sixth Wards as their very own—a symbol of status for those who had very little otherwise.

Historians point to Hamblin and the Bowery Theater in the 1830s as a pioneer in American dramatic theater. It helped create some of the very first "stars" that the country could call its own and launched the careers of actors like Junius Brutus Booth, father of Edwin and John Wilkes Booth, and Frank Chanfrau, the man who made the Bowery b'hoy character a nineteenth-century household name.

Bowery Theater audiences were treated to easy-to-follow, action-packed story lines and characters tantamount to today's "professional" wrestling—the villain, the hero, the comic relief—all carefully constructed to whip audiences into a frenzy by the time the good guy finally foils the bad guy in the third act. Ethnic stereotypes were played to the extreme, to the audience's delight, leaving no guessing on their part who to cheer for.

Though the practice of white actors donning black face paint and mimicking (their exaggerated version of) black culture dates back to the 1820s, it was at the Bowery Theater that blackface minstrelsy became popularized in the 1830s when New York–born actor Thomas Dartmouth Rice brought a character named Jim Crow to the stage. Rice was a struggling actor touring the Midwest and southern theater circuit in the 1820s when he encountered an elderly, crippled stable hand in Kentucky who became the inspiration for a satirical song and dance routine called "Jumping Jim Crow." Rice's soft-shoe shuffles and unflattering portrayals of blacks gained him popularity around the country before landing him a headlining slot at the Bowery Theater in 1832, which made him a bona fide star.

The success of "Jumping Jim Crow" inspired numerous minstrel acts across the country, but none achieved the success and notoriety of Rice's character.

Nos. 46–48 Bowery today. *Courtesy of Shirley Dluginski.*

The term "Jim Crow" would become synonymous with racial segregation in America over the next century and a half.

The Bowery Theater continued to reinvent itself for close to a century as the neighborhood experienced successive changes in population. By the Civil War, the theater catered to the Irish rowdies of the Five Points and Fourth Ward. In 1879, Atlantic Beer Garden owner William Kramer took possession of the building, renamed it the Thalia Theatre and reclaimed the institution's respectability. Here, critically acclaimed Germanic operas and plays were the standard until 1888, when the Thalia was subleased to a producer named Jacob who produced plays in Yiddish throughout the 1889–90 season. To follow was Italian opera at the turn of the century and Chinese vaudeville, until July 1929, when the theater burned down for its seventh and final time.

In the spring of 1931, the property at 46–48 Bowery, which also included the adjoining 16–20 Elizabeth Street, was sold by the city in a foreclosure sale. A May 1931 *New York Times* article states that the lot would be made into a parking garage, but by the 1950s it was home to various businesses like the Vaughn Barber School and Jewelry Exchange, and by the 1960s, it was referred to as the Canal Street Arcade (a sort of mini-mall hosting mostly Chinese merchants).

50–54 BOWERY

On January 19, 1855, two large fires destroyed nine old Bowery buildings, including nos. 52 and 54. The second fire of the night started in a shed attached to a lamp store at 52 Bowery and quickly spread to neighboring wooden buildings.

In 1858, a man named William Kramer combined 50, 52 and 54 Bowery into the largest and most successful German bier hall in the city, the Atlantic Beer Garden. The Atlantic Beer Garden was immense; holding more than two thousand people, it featured a saloon, restaurant, stage, lodging rooms, shooting gallery and bowling alleys, and even its own on-site brewery. By 1893, it also featured the largest orchestrion in the world. Built for the 1892 Chicago World's Fair and purchased soon after by the Atlantic, the instrument was twenty feet high and eighteen feet wide, with beautiful stenciled glass and sculpted cabinetry. It could mimic several instruments at the same time from a music roll that had to be accessed by climbing a built-in staircase.

As the neighborhood's German population declined, so did the popularity of the Atlantic Beer Garden. In July 1915, Kramer leased the building to John Miele for vaudeville performances and motion picture screenings, but it closed for good less than a decade later.

Inside Atlantic Beer Garden. *From* Harper's Weekly, *1871.*

54–58 Bowery

This very unique, stately, domed building at the southwest corner of Bowery and Canal Street was built in 1924 for the Citizen's Savings Bank (est. 1860), which moved here from its original location at no. 13 Avenue A in 1862.

When the Atlantic Beer Garden next door went out of business, Citizen's Bank expanded its property and hired architect Clarence W. Brazer to design the structure you see today. In July 1942, Citizen's merged with the Manhattan Savings Bank and then merged several more times over the years until 1999, when its current tenant, HSBC, moved in.

Bowery at Canal today, facing north. *Courtesy of Shirley Dluginski and Mitchell Grubler.*

75 Bowery

From 1790 to 1798, prominent silversmith Abraham Gerritze Forbes lived and worked at this address, then known as 75 Bowery Lane, where he crafted tea sets, spoons, trays and other silver goods. Over two hundred years later, silverware etched with the initials "AGF" is still fetching big bucks in auctions, like the pair of 1785 Forbes table spoons that can be found online for $300.

One of Forbes's apprentices at 75 Bowery was Garrett Eoff, a man who would go on to become a world-renowned craftsman. (Eoff's work can be seen today on exhibit at the Brooklyn Museum.)

This address appears to have housed a retail business almost consecutively for over the next two centuries, including the period of time it housed a brothel in the 1840s, according to a congressional report.

In December 1865, a fire broke out at a chair manufacturer at 71 Bowery, and within two hours it consumed almost every building along the Bowery between Canal and Hester Streets, stretching east to Christie Street. Six buildings were completely destroyed by the flames, and at least half a dozen others, including 75 Bowery, had to be rebuilt. Fire struck again in May 1870 when an incident in a tobacco factory caused the roof to collapse.

Yet another fire at 75 Bowery in 1891 caused a small riot when the awning of the Red Star furniture store caught fire and a fireman attempted to access the building via the lodging house next door. The problem was that the firefighter was not wearing a uniform, and a brawl ensued when residents could not identify him. The fire was extinguished by the time police showed up, but when they tried to arrest the lodgers, neighbors assaulted the police, and reinforcements had to be called to quell the situation. Just another night on the Bowery.

In 1929, 75 Bowery was home to the Jewelry Exchange, where in September of that year detectives recovered $200,000 in stolen jewelry, including a $10,000 bracelet stolen from millionaire Richard P. Weber during a home invasion a month earlier. Arresting officers were offered $15,000 bribes but turned them down.

This address no longer exists.

77–79 BOWERY

A popular, long-running, Yiddish-language newspaper, *Der Morgen Zhurnal* ("The Morning Journal"), was founded at this location in 1901 by a man named Jacob Sapirstein. It was the only morning daily newspaper at the time catering to the Conservative Jewish immigrant population of New York City, and it quickly gained popularity because it offered updated job listings and articles by correspondents reporting from Russia, Poland and the Balkans.

Der Morgen Zhurnal reached a circulation of 111,000 by 1916 and featured such respected writers as Elieizer Joseph Margoshes, Aleksander Mukdoyni (known as America's first prominent Yiddish theater critic) and Rabbi Milton

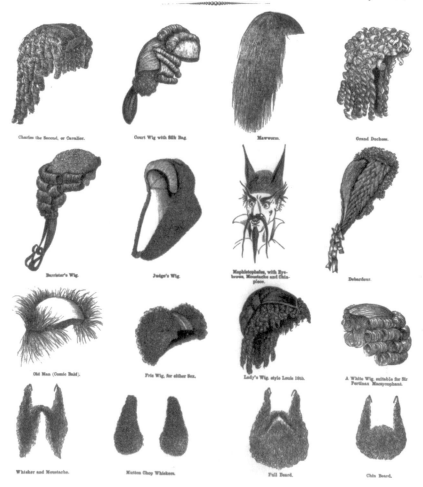

Theatrical Wigs and Beards ad, 100 Bowery, 1880. *Courtesy of Library of Congress.*

J. Rosen, an Orthodox Jewish U.S. Army chaplain who reported directly from the warzone at the height of the Korean War.

In 1904, Sapirstein went on to publish *Der Amirikaner* (known as the *Jewish American*), which was modeled after the *Saturday Evening Post* and advertised itself as a "preparatory school for the wanderer." It strived to teach Jewish immigrants "how to become real, true Americans."

In April 1935, thirty-two office workers at *Der Morgen Zhurnal* went on strike and staged several demonstrations in front of 75–79 Bowery, resulting in numerous arrests. Influential American author and editor H.L. Mencken addressed the disgruntled workers on May 1, lecturing them on the "futility and foolishness of strikes."

In the 1950s, *Der Morgen Zhurnal* merged with *Der Tog* ("The Day") to create the *Tog Morgen Zhurnal*, which continued publication until 1971.

99–101 BOWERY

In 1840, one of P.T. Barnum's first New York City businesses, a "shoe-blackening, cologne and bear's grease" store, was located at 101 Bowery. On June 4, 1838, Barnum returned to New York City after a failed theater company tour of the South where, in one instance, the company was chased from town at gunpoint by a local mob.

"Disgusted with the life of an itinerant showman," Barnum yearned for a "respectable, permanent business" and placed an ad in a local paper for a business partner, stating that he had $2,500 to invest. Ninety-three people responded: one-third were saloonkeepers, and the rest were a mixed bag of inventors, pawnbrokers, counterfeiters and scam artists. "Whoever wishes to buy a cheap dollar's worth of knowledge [on] how people live, or hope to live, let him spend that sum in advertising for a partner," Barnum states in his autobiography, *The Life of P.T. Barnum*.

After several failed interviews, Barnum finally settled on a man named Proler who manufactured "pasteblacking, water-proof paste for leather, Cologne water, and bear's grease." In the spring of 1839, the pair rented out 101 Bowery for $600 a year. Mr. Proler manufactured the products and Barnum kept accounts, managed advertising and attended to sales.

The co-partnership would not last long, as it was dissolved by January 1840 when Mr. Proler packed up and sailed for Rotterdam, leaving Barnum in debt and out of business. (Slight revenge was served when Barnum published the recipes to Mr. Proler's products.)

By the spring of 1840, Barnum had again tried his hand in show business when he leased the concert saloon at Vauxhall Gardens for a short time to produce small variety shows.

In May 1867, police raided an illegal faro parlor operating at 101 Bowery, arresting the proprietor, staff and twenty-two patrons. Faro is a European card game that became the most popular game of chance in American saloons and gambling parlors by the mid-nineteenth century. Based on simply guessing the dealer's next card, the game was simple to play—but just as easy to fix, leaving gambling houses at an extreme advantage.

The popularity of faro waned by the end of the Civil War; however, it was revived during the neighborhood's vice heyday of the 1890s as a game called "stuss." The only difference between faro and stuss is that the dealer draws cards from a stack in stuss, whereas faro cards are dealt from a mechanized box. Local gangs went to war over control of the multimillion-dollar stuss enterprise in New York City, which was centered on the Lower East Side.

By the late nineteenth century, 99–101 Bowery was home to Worth's Museum and Congress of Living and Inanimate Curiosities, a popular dime museum opened by E.M. Worth in September 1881. Children who brought a live mouse (presumably to feed one of the many live animals kept in the museum's menagerie) were admitted free and would be treated to such wonders as the finest specimen of Architeuthis—giant squid—in North America and what Worth claimed to be the preserved head of Charles Julius Guiteau, the man who assassinated President James A. Garfield in 1881.

On July 7, 1882, E.M. Worth was bitten by one of the fifty-four live rattlesnakes that were kept in a display case of the museum. Worth routinely fed the snakes raw meat after hours, which almost proved fatal on this occasion, as the bite sent him to the hospital in a "comatose condition." Worth survived the ordeal and is said to be the first person treated for a rattlesnake bite in New York City.

Worth's Museum moved to Sixth Avenue and Thirtieth Street by 1895, to a neighborhood known as the Tenderloin, where it would offer more refined entertainment and help launch the careers of early singer/songwriters like Robert Cole.

By the 1890s, 99–101 Bowery was home to the Alder Theatre, where in 1894, notable anarchist Johan Most addressed a crowd of Russian nihilists to praise the murder of a Russian emperor: "I am somewhat at a loss as to whether I should praise God for the death of the Czar Alexander III or to give thanks to the devil," Most said. Contemporary J. Gordin then announced, "We hope to rejoice within a year over the death of Nicolas II."

103–105 Bowery

No. 103–105 Bowery is the site of the George B. Bunnell's New American Museum, where the "dime museum" format is said to have been popularized.

Outside a Bowery dime museum. *From* Darkness and Daylight: Or, Lights and Shadows of New York Life, *by Helen Campbell, Thomas Wallace Knox and Thomas Byrnes, 1895.*

Previous page: Inside a Bowery dime museum. *From* Darkness and Daylight: Or, Lights and Shadows of New York Life, *by Helen Campbell, Thomas Wallace Knox and Thomas Byrnes, 1895.*

Though curiosity exhibits were fairly common by 1876, Bunnell, a former assistant to P.T. Barnum, is credited with combining the museum, live performance and ten-cent admission policy that made these centers of amusement so popular among the working class by the end of the century. The combination wax museum, circus sideshow and live theater thrilled audiences who flocked to see "mermaids" (dead manatees), mutated animals, dwarves and giants, amputees, snake charmers, mentalists, ventriloquists, sword swallowers and the like, as well as live vaudeville, burlesque and minstrel skits.

Bunnell's museum, opened in the fall of 1876, occupied the first three floors of 103–105 Bowery, with each level divided into two large rooms. The first floor housed the "Theatorium," a large hall where live performances and special exhibitions took place. The second floor housed a menagerie of exotic live animals, and the third floor was dedicated to "freaks," such as the tattooed man and the "two-brained" baby. One popular room called "Dante's Inferno" was made up to depict hell with wax effigies of disgraced public figures like William "Boss" Tweed. Other New American Museum favorites were the

six-hundred-pound "Fat Boy," the forty-five-pound "Living Skeleton" and the "Leopard Boy" (more than likely a black boy with vitiligo).

The New American Museum occupied this address for two years before moving to a new location at 298 Bowery, where it remained until a fire destroyed that building in June 1879.

Over the next decade, 103 and 105 Bowery would become home to a pair of the most notoriously ornery saloons in New York City, operated by some of its most notoriously ornery characters like "Owney" Geoghegan, Michael McGlory and John J. Flynn.

The most noted of the lot is Owen "Owney" Geoghegan (pronounced "gay-gen,") an Irish-born professional pugilist and career criminal who had earned the reputation as one of the toughest men in the city (a measure of status in the slums). Geoghegan arrived in New York City with his family in 1849 at about ten years old. As a boy he took on fights along the East River to earn money and eventually stepped into the pro ring to fight

Top: Jo-Jo, billed as "King of Dog-Faced Freaks." *From* The Illustrated American, *1890.*

Bottom: The Murays triplets were popular performers of the era.

Geoghegan is in good company in this 1861 magazine ad. *From* American Athlete Journal.

(and defeat) such toughs as James McGarum, Con Orem and Ed Tuohey, earning a championship title that he held from 1861 to 1864. Using money he won in the ring, Geoghegan opened a "sporting house" on First Avenue and Twenty-first Street that became headquarters of the powerful Gashouse Gang.

His saloon on the Bowery opened in the mid-1870s under the name the Burnt Rag, but it was also referred to as Owney's Night House and featured a twelve-foot-wide boxing ring on each of its two floors, where contestants could battle it out for a five-dollar prize.

Geoghegan was soon recruited into politics as a "ward healer"—someone who "motivates" voters—where his fearless nature earned him much respect among corrupt politicos, who in turn helped keep Geoghegan out of jail for most of his career. In one incident, Geoghegan was successful in having a pesky local police captain removed from the district and flaunted this fact with a very public mock funeral for the officer at his saloon.

In January 1878, Geoghegan shot and killed a man named James "Jim Rose" Morton during a dispute at this address. Geoghegan fled but later turned himself in, and his charges were eventually dismissed. In December 1878, Geoghegan was arrested again for shooting two patrons who argued over the price of a drink, but the case was dismissed when it was claimed that Geoghegan acted in self-defense.

The law finally caught up with Owen "Owney" Geoghegan in the spring of 1883 when the Society for the Prevention of Cruelty to Children had him arrested for allowing a ten-year-old boy to frequent his bar. Geoghegan was sentenced to prison, where it is said his health deteriorated. Upon release, Geoghegan moved to Hot Springs, Arkansas, to recover, but he died of natural causes in January 1885. His body was returned to New York City, where hundreds of people turned out for his funeral, including several politicians, prize fighters and local celebrities.

104–106 BOWERY

This address has been through several incarnations since the mid-nineteenth century, when it was known as the National Theater, a popular working-class entertainment venue that charged only twenty cents admission and offered four hours of entertainment each night.

The National is perhaps most notable for hosting one of the earliest stage productions of Harriet Beecher Stowe's bestselling antislavery novel, *Uncle*

Tom's Cabin, which premiered at the National Theater on July 18, 1853. The stage production was brought to New York City by George L. Altken shortly after a three-month run in Troy, New York.

Altken's production is thought of as being one of the first to stay true to the antislavery theme at the heart of Beecher's novel—at a time before copyright protection—when other productions took the liberty of watering down the trials and tribulations of the main character, an elderly slave named Uncle Tom.

The *New York Times* reported on the stage premiere at the National Theater and the surprisingly receptive Bowery audience who, "with tearful eyes and enthusiastic cheers, acknowledged the grand sentiment of humanity contained in it."

By 1875, 104–106 Bowery was home to the International Garden Saloon and then the National Garden before a group of Romanian Jewish actors arrived in New York and opened the Roumanian Opera House in 1886. It was one of the earliest Yiddish theater playhouses in America and home to some of its earliest stars.

On September 6, 1896, when the establishment was operating under the name of the Liberty Theater, police interrupted the first act of the Italian play *Santarella* and arrested its two lead actors, twenty-six-year-old Antonio Maiori and fifty-six-year-old Anetta Zaccone, for wearing a nun and priest costume in violation of the "theatrical law." (Maiori would go on to become one of the most respected actors in American theater.)

The Nickelodeon Theatre occupied the premises in 1897 and offered a popular weekly amateur night, where a packed house of rowdies would make or break hopeful comedians, singers, dancers and musicians. How rowdy? The theater's tag line was, "No amusement temple in the country better provided with exits."

In November 1898, 104–106 Bowery was destroyed by a three-alarm fire but was quickly rebuilt as the Manhattan Music Hall, owned and operated by 260-pound bail bondsman and City Alderman Frederick F. Fleck, a Tim Sullivan crony on the Tammany Hall payroll. Fleck was a boorish, arrogant, larger-than-life character whose self-importance made him famous throughout the local wards. His theater catered to a somewhat upscale crowd where prostitutes worked the curtained boxes and galleries upstairs (patrons who wanted to stay had to purchase drinks at a whopping one dollar per round), where it is said Fleck would look down from the balcony and "carefully scrutinize" his guests on the lower floor.

In April 1901, the Committee of Fifteen targeted the Manhattan Music Hall as part of a multi-venue crackdown on vice in the Bowery district. Fleck was not present at the time of the raid, and the committee believed he was

Nos. 104–106 Bowery today. *Courtesy of Shirley Dluginski.*

tipped off in advance of the impending trouble. Once they caught up with him, Fleck reacted with his usual brutishness. One committee member said Fleck's conduct and language were "the worst that he had ever encountered," using expressions "too vile for publication." Fleck was charged with maintaining a disorderly house, but despite eyewitness testimony, his political connections got him acquitted on May 28 of that year.

By 1904, a Yiddish theater named People's Music Hall occupied 104–106 Bowery. This is the first business at this address that appears to have a registered telephone number, "4616-spring."

Over half a century of theatrical history would come to an end by the 1930s, when a lodging house moved into 104–106 Bowery that lasted well into the 1990s.

113 BOWERY

In the 1850s and '60s, 113 Bowery was home to Union Hall, assembly rooms for political associations like the Independent Democratic General Committee and the German Democratic Central Club, which met here on

November 22, 1861, to nominate C. Godfrey Gunther as their candidate for mayor in the 1861 election. Gunther, a Tammany politician and darling of the German community, lost to Republican George Opdyke that year but would run again and be elected in 1863, serving his term as mayor of New York City through 1866.

By the 1870s, Union Hall became known as Bowery Garden Theatre, described as a "long, narrow beer hall with a little bit of a stage," which offered a variety of standard lowbrow Bowery fare for twenty-five-cent admission.

In the winter of 1882, all of the beer tables were removed and replaced with theater seats when brothers Leon and Myron Golubok moved in and opened the first venue dedicated to Yiddish theater in America. The Golubok brothers introduced Yiddish theater to the United States in August 1882 at Turn Halle on East Fourth Street, where they brought a small European theater troupe and paired them with local talent Boris Thomashefsky and Israel Barsky for a production of Abraham Goldfaden's *Season of the Witch*. The troupe would take over the Bowery Garden Theatre later that year and offer productions like Paysach Thomashefsky's *Rothschild's Biography* and Barsky's *The Madwoman* (said to be the first Yiddish play written in America).

The company did not last long, however, as internal feuds and financial problems split the troupe into two factions by 1883. Neither of the new groups found immediate success, so the Goluboks moved to Chicago, and Thomashefsky tried his hand in Philadelphia for three years before returning to New York City to become a Yiddish theater star.

No. 113 Bowery would not sit empty for long, as a new professional theater troupe from Europe calling themselves the Russian Yiddish Opera Company would turn the Bowery Garden into the Oriental Theatre by the end of 1883. Led by playwright Joseph Lateiner, the Oriental at first produced plays with biblical themes, like *Esther and Haman* and *Joseph and His Brothers*, but soon turned to more contemporary titles, such as the popular *Immigration to America*.

Within a few years, the Oriental began to face stiff competition as the popularity of Yiddish theater grew among the city's immigrant population and New York started attracting more seasoned actors from overseas. (Also, the Czar of Russia outlawed Yiddish theatre in 1883.) When Sigmund Mogulesco (or Mogulescu) and his troupe arrived in America in 1886, they opened the Roumanian Opera House right across the street from the Oriental. The first major rivalry between Yiddish theater companies in the United States began, and the two theaters went to war over patronage. If the Roumanian produced *King Solomon*, the Oriental would run *Solomon's*

Trial; if the Oriental booked a popular artist, the Roumanian would counter with a better offer. And so it went until the 1880s, when the Oriental ran into a couple of speed bumps, like in January 1886, when the city refused to renew the theater's liquor license, and in June 1888, when it was cited by the New York Society for the Prevention of Cruelty to Children for using underage actors in stage productions.

By the end of the century, 113 Bowery had been re-launched as the New London Theatre, but it retained none of its cultural or artistic spirit (the *New York Times* described the New London as a "vile dive"). In April 1891, an intoxicated patron named Albert Stoll shot a performer named Kittie Dunsworth in self-defense and then himself out of sheer drunkenness. According to reports, Dunsworth tried to rob Stoll when he pulled out a revolver and shot out seven of her teeth before turning the gun on himself. Both survived.

On February 28, 1904, a fire that started in a carpet manufacturer on the second and third floor caused a commotion as firefighters battled the blaze from atop the Third Avenue elevated train platform. At one point, the main water hose feeding the firefighters burst and, "to the intense amusement of the spectators in the street," several stranded rail cars got soaked (along with the crowds of rush hour commuters packed inside them).

114 BOWERY

The first floor of this building was once occupied by a saloon owned by the legendary Steve Brodie, a man whose claim to fame was just that, a claim, that in 1886 he jumped from the Brooklyn Bridge and survived.

Brodie, a native Lower East Sider, was an outgoing, blusterous youth who earned the nicknames "Napoleon of Newsboys" and "George Washington of Bootblackers" because of the influence he had over other boys in the rowdy Fourth Ward. (Think Christian Bale in the 1992 movie-musical *Newsies*.) In one 1879 interview, sixteen-year-old Steve Brodie bragged about how he and other local "newsies" would band together to chase new competition out of their territory and complained about how Italians were taking all the bootblacking jobs.

A professional gambler as a young adult, Brodie fell into debt when he took on a dare to jump off the New York City landmark for $200—just months after daredevil Robert Odlum was killed while attempting the same stunt. As

Above: Gum vendors, 1910. *Courtesy of Library of Congress.*

Right: Steve Brodie poster. *Courtesy of Library of Congress.*

No. 114 Bowery today. *Courtesy of Shirley Dluginski.*

Bowery at Grand Street, circa 1900. *Courtesy of Library of Congress.*

Brodie began to take full advantage of the publicity around his planned jump, a liquor dealer named Moritz Herzber offered to finance a saloon in Brodie's name—if he survived.

On the morning of July 23, 1886, Brodie stood on the railing of the bridge while a couple of friends tested the waters below in a rowboat and news reporters gathered on a pier nearby. At 10:00 a.m., Brodie's team called off the jump, claiming the tide was too strong. Brodie came down from the structure only to return about 2:00 p.m. that day, when it is claimed he rode in the back of a wagon until he got about one hundred yards over the bridge, at which point he took off his hat and shoes and plunged over the railing into the East River.

Despite several "eyewitnesses" and lengthy news reports, most historians believe the jump was a hoax, theorizing that a friend threw a life-size dummy from the wagon that people mistook for Brodie amidst all the excitement. Brodie was arrested after being "rescued" from the water, but charges were dropped and he became an instant celebrity. Herzber made good on his promise, and Brodie's saloon was opened at 114 Bowery. It also doubled as a museum dedicated to the stunt.

The public could not get enough of Steve Brodie, who went on to tour the country in vaudeville musicals *Mad Money* and *On the Bowery*, re-creating his famous leap for clamoring fans. Eventually, Brodie settled in Buffalo, New York, where he died from diabetes in 1901 at the young age of thirty-nine.

Steve Brodie's stunt inspired a slew of pop culture references, including the 1933 Hollywood film *The Bowery*, in which fellow Lower East Sider George Raft portrayed Brodie in the lead role; and a 1949 Looney Tunes cartoon named *Bowery Bugs*, which re-imagines Bugs Bunny being the motivation for Brodie's jump. The urban legend also inspired a popular saying: "pulling a Brodie."

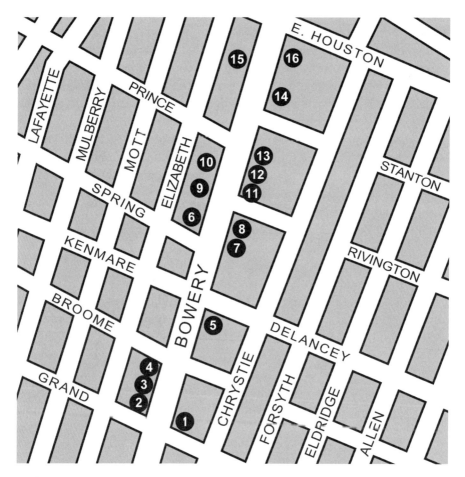

Addresses discussed in this chapter. *Courtesy of Lower East Side History Project.*

Chapter 3

Grand Street to East Houston Street

129 Bowery

Former vice president, suspected U.S. conspirator and Founding Father killer Aaron Burr lived at this address in 1833 with his illegitimate son after a failed marriage to former prostitute and Napoleon sympathizer Eliza Jumel.

No, that is not a headline from a supermarket weekly. A seventy-seven-year-old ailing Aaron Burr moved into 129 Bowery when a four-month relationship (his second marriage) went south. This was the home and business of a jeweler named Aaron Columbus Burr. Depending on the source, Aaron C. Burr is referred to as either the "adopted" or "probably illegitimate" son of the ex-politician, who is perhaps most famous for killing Alexander Hamilton in an 1804 pistol duel.

By the time the elder Burr lived at this address, he was running out of money, partially paralyzed and had bounced around from one Lower Manhattan residence to another. After his short stint at 129 Bowery, a Scottish housekeeper took care of Burr at her residence on Broadway for a short time before his final move to Staten Island, where he died in September 1836.

Aaron Columbus Burr, who sold upscale handmade jewelry from his store at this address, was, according to an obituary, born in France in 1808 to Count Verdi de Lisie. In 1816, he traveled to America under the care of Aaron Burr to continue his education. When the count died soon after, Burr adopted him. At least, that is the story they are sticking to.

Younger Burr was also a lawyer and New York City constable in his early days, holding the title of "Superintendent of Lights and Gas" in the 1840s. By the 1850s, Aaron C. Burr had established himself as a prominent businessman and became active in political lobbying. During the Civil War, Burr and a friend named Anna Ella Carroll, a close adviser to President Abraham Lincoln, tried to persuade the commander in chief to colonize the freed slaves of British Honduras (now Belize). Lincoln decided against it, but Burr established the American Honduras Company to capitalize on mahogany exports. He retired by 1862 a wealthy man and passed away in 1882 at his residence on 121st Street.

130 Bowery

This elegant construct was built for the Bowery Savings Bank in 1895 by renowned architect Stanford White, the man behind some of New York City's most revered landmarks, such as the second Madison Square Garden, several libraries and the Washington Square Arch. The thirty-six-thousand-

Bowery Savings Bank, 1898. *Courtesy of Library of Congress.*

square-foot interior features sixty-five-foot ceilings topped with an amber glass skylight, marble floors, Corinthian columns and Venetian glass. The limestone exterior was designed in the stately Beaux Arts style, with sculptures by artist Frederick MacMonnies adorning the pediment.

The Bowery Savings Bank was incorporated at this location on May 1, 1834, as one of the earliest savings banks in New York, an institution originally created to finance the Erie Canal. Lasting a full century and a half, the bank went under in the 1980s after several mergers and name changes. In 1987, the building was sold for $200 million. Today, the interior functions as an upscale event hall, hosting parties, weddings, banquets, celebrity functions and even boxing matches.

As of this writing, a company named Racebrook Capital is preparing to auction 150 "Timeless Trademarks and Domain Names" at the Waldorf Astoria, including "Bowery Savings Bank."

No. 130 Bowery is listed on the National Register of Historic Places.

138 Bowery

In 1903 and 1904, this address was home to Drammatico Nazionale, a popular Italian theater under the management of Antonio Maiori. The notable companies of Enrico Costantini and Francsesco Vela also performed during the two years the Nazionale existed.

It can be argued that Italian American theater began in New York City in 1808, when Mozart's librettist, Lorenzo Da Ponte, (a man whose first job in America was as a grocer on the Bowery), recruited Columbia University students to stage small Italian plays and operas like Vittorio Alfieri's *Mirra*. However, it wasn't until the 1870s that Italians and Sicilians would arrive in large numbers and organize amateur and professional theater clubs. Contrary to popular belief, not all immigrants were uneducated. Many intellectuals and artisans wound up in Italian colonies of the Unites States, and many were drawn to the theater world.

In the early years, these immigrant and first-generation actors, playwrights and producers catered exclusively to the Italian communities, translating classics into regional dialects and developing new productions relating to the immigrant experience. One of the earliest of these professional companies was the Il Circolo Filodrammatico Italo-Americano (the Italian American Amateur Theater Club), which caused a small sensation in 1880 when it performed *Maria Giovanna* at Dramatic Hall on East Houston Street.

The foreign themes of these otherwise world-class plays and operettas kept mainstream success out of reach for many years. After decades in the shadows of German theatrical companies, Italian theater got a boost by the turn of the century with the success of such actors as Antonio Maiori, who earned the respect of high-society theater circles by commanding such roles as Shylock in *The Merchant of Venice*.

Sicilian-born Maiori arrived in New York City in 1892 at the age of twenty-four. By 1895, the studied actor made waves producing small plays in an old row house at 24 Spring Street (less than two blocks from the Bowery), where his Shakespearean productions thrilled packed houses and caught the attention of critics and theater managers.

By 1903, the time he operated out of 138 Bowery, Maiori was one of the most celebrated actors in New York City. He went on to open and manage several theaters and enjoy a successful career, inspiring many twentieth-century entertainers. One year before his death in 1838, Maiori founded the Italian Actors Union, today known as the Guild of Italian American Actors.

Other local actors, actresses, producers and playwrights helped to shape Italian American theater in the States, including Eduardo Migliaccio, Pasquale Rapone, Esterina Cunico and Maiori's wife, Concetta Arcamone, to name a very few.

By the 1910s, the Bowery was at the heart of the Italian theater district, and three of its most important venues were located here: Maiori's Royal Theatre (235–237 Bowery), Teatro Italiano de Varieta (273 Bowery) and Acierno's Italian Theatre (46–48 Bowery), which offered "grand operas" for twenty-five cents to a dollar and dramas for five to twenty-five cents.

148 BOWERY

This address, which is 341 Broome Street officially, is said to be the oldest continuously operated hotel in New York City, possibly dating back to 1805. It has operated under names like New Bull's Head, the Westchester, Commercial, Occidental, Pioneer (which for a short time operated as a homeless shelter for women in the 1970s) and, today, the SoHotel.

A series of Italian restaurants occupied the first floor in the early twentieth century, including the Tripoli in 1914 and the Italian Garden by 1916, where on October 5 of that year, (Sicilian) Morello Gang member Giuseppe "Big

Man" Verrazano was gunned down by assassins sent by Brooklyn's (Neapolitan) crime boss, Pellegrino Morano. As Verrazano dined, two men walked in and opened fire, killing their target and wounding two other patrons.

Verrazano was a marked man. He was originally going to be killed alongside Nicolas Morello and "Charles" Ubriaco during an ambush in Brooklyn on September 7, 1916, but Verrazano did not make the trip for some reason, so Morano sent his men to the Bowery to finish the job.

This killing was part of a larger war between the Sicilian and Neapolitan gangs, which fought for control of various gambling and extortion rackets in Manhattan and Brooklyn early in the century. Neapolitan Camorra boss Pellegrino Morano was convicted of the September 7 murders and deported back to Italy by 1919. In Morano's absence, the Sicilian Mafia got the upper hand in the war, and eventually any Camorra who did not fold into a Sicilian organization was put out of business—permanently.

165–167 Bowery

This address was home to Miner's Bowery Theater, an important venue in the evolution of American variety and vaudeville entertainment.

Miner's Bowery Theater was owned and operated by Henry "Harry" Clay Miner, a native New Yorker, ex–municipal police officer, ex–volunteer firefighter and graduate of the College of Physicians and Surgeons, where he earned a pharmaceutical degree. After college, Harry tried several odd jobs to support his family and eventually began a career in entertainment as an agent for traveling acts Wild Bill Hickok, Buffalo Bill and Texas Jack, among others.

Harry Miner staked his claim on the Bowery in early 1876 by purchasing a store at the corner of Bowery and Spring called Dr. Brown's Pharmacy, which dated back to 1804. In November 1876, Miner partnered with a man named Jim Donaldson and opened the London Theatre at 235 Bowery. But by 1878, Miner sold his interest in the London and purchased this old building at 165–167, renovated it and opened his own playhouse—the first of many Miner (and eventually his family) would go on to own in this city and others, inventing the idea of "chain theaters."

Miner's Bowery Theater at 165–167 Bowery was a widely popular venue and launching pad for the careers of many future stars, including Eddie Cantor, Weber and Fields and the Four Cohans. It pioneered the "amateur night" format, made famous later by the Apollo in Harlem and other theaters. "The hook"— arguably the most recognizable symbol of American vaudeville—was invented here in 1902. The tradition of the "hook" is said to have started on a busy Friday amateur night when the crowd grew increasingly restless during a solo performance. Miner's son, Tom Miner, urged stage manager Charles Guthinger to fasten a leftover stage prop—a wooden cane—to a pole and yank the aspiring tenor off stage from behind the curtain. From then on, if a performer offended the audience, they would start shouting, "Get the hook!" and the custom was adopted.

Harry Miner's innovation went beyond the stage. He founded the Springer Lithography Company by 1880, which provided him with all the in-house printing and promotional materials he needed, and he also invested in newspapers and other small businesses.

Inside the theater, which also housed a saloon and poolroom, burly security guards would patrol each floor to survey the audience for any signs of trouble. It was common for performances to get raucous, and the entertainers dished it out as much as they took it. The few rules at Miner's included: no spitting tobacco, no throwing objects and no harassing women. Any of these offenses could earn you a rough landing on the Bowery sidewalk.

By the 1890s, Miner was a millionaire and one of New York City's most prominent businessmen. He had developed influential political allies and

Nos. 165–167 Bowery today. *Courtesy of Shirley Dluginski.*

helped introduce friend and politician "Big" Tim Sullivan to the theater world, in which Sullivan became a large investor. In return, Sullivan helped keep the law off of Miner's back.

Miner took advantage of his popularity and clout and ran for Congress on the Democratic ticket in 1892, which he won. He also became president of the Actors Fund of America in 1893.

Henry Clay Miner died in 1900, and his sons took over operation of all his businesses and properties. Miner's Theater at 165–167 Bowery lasted until about 1905, when Maiori's Royal Theatre took over the premises and transformed the address into an Italian playhouse.

No. 165–167 Bowery's theatrical history ended in the 1920s, when it operated as the Crystal Hotel (as the name still suggests on the façade), until a string of retail and wholesalers began a half century–plus run in the 1940s.

190 Bowery

This impressive, landmarked, six-story Beaux Arts–style building was built in 1898 and designed by architect Robert Maynicke for the Germania Bank of

No. 190 Bowery today. *Courtesy of Shirley Dluginski.*

New York City. The institution was founded in 1869 at no. 185 Bowery but was moved to this location three decades later to accommodate its expansion.

Photographer Jay Maisel purchased the building in 1966 for $102,000 and renovated the old bank into a seventy-two-room, thirty-five-thousand-square-foot family home, studio and office—worth tens of millions of dollars today.

No. 190 Bowery was designated a landmark in 2005.

199–201 BOWERY

This address has a long theatrical history starting on August 5, 1858, when Hoym's Theatre opened its doors with a troupe that included dancer Louise Lamoureux. The theater, named after owner Otto Von Hoym, went through several owners, formats and managerial changes over the next few years, until Samuel S. Sharpley was hired in June 1865. In July of that year, new manager "Sam" Sharpley, who had a minstrel company of his own called the Ironclad Minstrels, booked a variety troupe led by actor and singer Tony Pastor for a short run at the Hoym.

Tony Pastor was a seasoned entertainer who began performing at age six or seven for the Hand in Hand Society, a temperance organization that lured followers with wholesome song and dance in lieu of lengthy sermons. He went on to build an impressive résumé performing in minstrel, variety and circus shows around the country, earning the reputation as a competent and likable singer and showman. Pastor's troupe performed at 199–201 Bowery on the last stop of a Northeast tour. The program was such a huge success that Sharpley and Pastor decided to form a partnership and purchase the theater from owner Richard M. Hooley, renaming it Tony Pastor's Opera House.

Sharpley retired after the first season, which ended on June 9, 1866, leaving the entire operation in Pastor's hands. The first few years were rough going; most of the respectable theaters had moved from the Bowery to the Fourteenth Street/Union Square district, and Pastor had a hard time drawing people to his venue. He experimented with several formats, promotions and giveaways but soon reached a formula that worked: clean, innocuous variety skits featuring comedy, singing, juggling, magic and so on, coupled with the banning of alcohol, smoking, obscenity and rowdy behavior. Pastor managed to attract women and middle-class families—a format the term "vaudeville" would become associated with from then on.

The *New York Times* wrote about Tony Pastor's Opera House in 1867, calling it "the acknowledged vaudeville house in the metropolis" and "the resort most cherished by ladies, children and the cultured mass of amusement seekers."

The word "vaudeville" derives from the Old French *vaudivire*, a shortening of *chanson du Vau de Vire* ("song of the Valley of Vire")—inspired by the fifteenth-century satirical folk songs of a valley in Calvados, Normandy, named Vire. By the eighteenth century, the term had become commonplace in music composition, describing a song in which different singers take turns singing a verse.

"Vaudeville" has been used to describe bawdy variety shows in America since the 1830s. Some historians believe it was selected essentially because it sounded fancy. Author of *American Vaudeville as Ritual*, Albert F. McLean suggests that the name was chosen "for its vagueness, its faint, but harmless exoticism, and perhaps its connotation of gentility." But Tony Pastor was the first to successfully package it as family entertainment.

Tony Pastor moved his theater to 585–587 Broadway in 1875 and remained there until 1881, when Tony Pastor's Opera House made its final move to the "respectable" theater district on East Fourteenth Street.

When an 1883 fire destroyed the building at 199–201 Bowery, Henry Clay Miner purchased the lot and built the 2,500-seat Miner's People's Theatre, which opened on September 3 of that year. For the next decade and a half, the People's Theatre continued as a "combination house," offering a mixed bag of minstrels, variety and sideshows alongside more serious theater like *Dr. Jekyll and Mr. Hyde* and *Tom Sawyer*.

In 1885, the People's Theatre earned the distinction of becoming the first playhouse in New York to be lit by electric light. Miner had an "isolated electric plant" installed in the building, and cables were laid under the street by the Edison Company to reach Miner's two other Bowery businesses (the drugstore and the Bowery Theater). Most theaters would remain gas lit for another decade until electricity was more widely distributed, at which time, according to the *Edison Monthly*, many started competing to feature the most elaborate light shows and stage productions, often at the expense of the actors.

In 1899, Jacob Adler and Boris Thomashefsky took over the People's Theatre at 199–201 Bowery and reopened it as a Yiddish playhouse (with a contract stipulating that the two would never perform on the same night). The two actors by this time had critics outside of the Yiddish theater world buzzing and were on the verge of breaking ethnic and class barriers, but they did not always get along well. By the end of the first season, Thomashefsky offered Adler $10,000 to never perform in New York again. This only made

Adler work harder and attempt what few actors would dare: a stage production of the laborious and ambitious *The Power of Darkness* by Leo Tolstoy, which Adler translated to Yiddish himself and appeared in as the character Nikita.

Opening night was met with a thunderous standing ovation and critical acclaim from the uptown critics who were in attendance to get a glimpse at the rising star tackle such a difficult role. Adler's performance was so moving, Thomashefsky was said to shed a tear as the two rejoiced backstage. Henry Thyrel wrote in *Theatre Magazine*, "If Adler could perform in English in a Broadway theatre he would be idolized." (Adler would get his chance to perform on Broadway in 1904.)

The People's Theatre was not exclusive to Yiddish performances. Jewish actors had formed a bond by the end of the century with Italian theater companies, which had no large, professional theater of their own at the time. Adler and Thomashefsky leased space to actors like Antonio Maiori, considered their contemporaries in Italian theater, and the companies shared sets and costumes and attended each other's performances.

In 1904, Adler had the Grand Theatre built on Bowery and Canal Street, which was dedicated to only Yiddish theater productions. The People's Theatre lasted well into the 1920s, and Thomashefsky established the National Yiddish Theatre Folksbiene in 1915; it still exists today.

207 BOWERY

From May 9, 1859, until May 14, 1862, this address was the headquarters of the John Hancock Lodge No. 70 of the Free and Accepted Masons, today known as the Hancock-Adelphi Dirigo Lodge No. 23. By 1868, offices and classrooms of the New-York Juvenile Guardian Society, an industrial school that assisted over seven hundred neighborhood children, were located here before moving to 101 St. Marks Place in 1876.

By the late 1880s, 207 Bowery had been purchased by theater mogul Henry C. Miner (who also owned the adjacent 201–203 and 205 Bowery), and he turned it into the People's Assembly Rooms, where organizations like the Knights of Labor would meet and concerts were held.

In December 1892, Miner dedicated 207 Bowery to the Comanche Club, to be used as headquarters for Tammany Hall's Third Assembly District representatives. That same year, "Big" Tim Sullivan was appointed as district leader and operated out of 207 Bowery. Within two years, he served his first term as state senator before being elected to Congress. This address served as the base camp for the Tim Sullivan Association throughout his political career, which spanned one of the most iniquitous eras in New York City history.

Timothy Daniel Sullivan (July 23, 1862–August 31, 1913), born and raised in the slums of the Five Points, was a widely popular politician who could mobilize voters en masse like none other since. He is often credited with streamlining the use of organized street gangs and the art of political graft—but more than that, he was a people's politician who stayed close to his working-poor roots.

However self-serving, Sullivan's philanthropic efforts are legendary; he was a master at securing votes and currying favors from prominent business leaders and Bowery vagrants alike. He recruited and worked closely with Jewish and Italian immigrant community leaders, bringing these underrepresented ethnic groups into the political fold for the first time since establishing themselves in the city.

Sullivan would visit local jails to pay bail for petty criminals, drunks and random vagrants and even personally accompany men to job sites to ensure they got work. He would donate enormous amounts of money, food and goods to local lodging houses and missions and regularly throw extravagant parties, parades and fireworks shows for the people of his district.

Every Christmas, hundreds of men would line up outside of 207 Bowery to wait for the doors to open at 8:00 a.m., when Sullivan would personally greet his guests with a handshake and a smile. Inside, they would walk through a hallway, past ornamental lamps with the words "Big Fellow" (Sullivan's nickname) engraved in gold and into a hall, where they would line up in rows to await the festivities. The guests would be entertained by live vaudeville performances, drink as much beer as they wanted and dine on a turkey meal with all the fixings—served by local congressmen, aldermen and judges. By 1902, a new tradition of giving out free shoes at Christmas dinner drew thousands of men each year who would line up for blocks.

Each Labor Day, Sullivan hosted an all-day event called a "chowder," which included three meals, entertainment, sporting contests and fireworks. Up to six thousand men would meet in front of 207 Bowery and march to the East River to awaiting ferryboats, which would take them to places like Donnelly's Grove (College Point) or Harlem River Park, where they would party until the wee hours of the morning.

However, the "Big Fellow" did not get where he was by being a nice guy. Unlike local politicos before him, Sullivan did not pander to the established conservative elite and allowed vice to thrive in his district. He contracted the services of gangsters like Paul Kelly and Monk Eastman, who assisted in voter fraud and keeping order among the criminals of Lower Manhattan (or attempted to at least). The Bowery district of the 1890s was filled with more gambling parlors, brothels, opium dens and illegal social clubs than perhaps any other time in history, largely due to Sullivan's influence. A 1909 *Cosmopolitan* magazine points to Sullivan as "the most scandalous individual in the pool-room (horse-gambling) grift in the United States."

By 1897, 207 Bowery had become known as the Metamora Club, where on February 19 of that year a new "Mayor of the Bowery"—sixty-five-year-old William "Fish Bill" Van Sicklen—was inducted into "office" by the district's most esteemed politicos and businessmen. In attendance were several judges, congressmen and then Senator Tim Sullivan, who awarded Van Sicklen a "key to the Bowery." Mayors were usually established businessmen of the district with proven loyalty to the Tammany machine. Van Sicklen was a lifelong Bowery resident, ex–volunteer firefighter and business owner at the Fulton Street Fish Market (hence the name "Fish Bill").

When Tim Sullivan died on August 31, 1913, his body lay in waiting at the Tim Sullivan Association headquarters, and over fifty thousand mourners passed by 207 Bowery to pay their respects. His coffin was propped up on two chairs in the assembly room on the fourth floor, which was covered with a multitude of candles and flowers.

Upon Sullivan's death, a rift formed within the Tim Sullivan Association as Tim's brother, Patrick "Paddy" Sullivan, fought for control of the organization (and position as Third Assembly District leader) against incumbent Alderman John J. White (born Giovanni Bianchi). During the power struggle, Paddy and his supporters moved to 259 Bowery in May 1914, while White's clan stayed at 207 Bowery.

White was reelected over Sullivan in 1915, but according to the *New York Times*, he retired the following year to pursue real estate interests, leaving the door open for Paddy Sullivan to take the position by 1916, which he would hold on to for only a short time.

By 1920, 207 Bowery had changed hands, was remodeled and rented out as retail space.

216 BOWERY

This address was home to John and Lydia Brown, who arrived from Ireland in the late eighteenth century to start a new life and settled on Bowery Lane. John built a twenty- by twenty-five-foot house on this site by hand and eventually opened a nearby porterhouse. The Browns had a daughter in 1798, Lydia Brown-Wheelock, who remained in the house for almost forty years. Young Lydia married an Irishman named Charles Wheelock who boarded at her parents' porterhouse, and they had eight children at 216 Bowery before moving to Ulysses, New York, in 1839.

One of the children born and raised here was Edwin Miller Wheelock, born August 30, 1829, who attended the Harvard Divinity School and was ordained as a Unitarian minister in 1857. Edwin became a highly respected reverend, speaker, author and outspoken critic against slavery. When he served as chaplain for New Hampshire's Fifteenth Regiment during the Civil War, he volunteered to face the battle head-on with the 128-man United States Colored Troops division of that state. After the war, Edwin became the very first superintendent of freedman schools in Texas, where, by 1865, he had

Top: Lydia Brown-Wheelock, 1798–February 6, 1872. *Courtesy of Sandy Smith.*

Bottom: Edwin Miller Wheelock, August 30, 1829–October 29, 1901. *Courtesy of Sandy Smith.*

Above: One-mile marker in front of 214–216 Bowery, circa 1908. *Courtesy of the Green-Wood Historic Fund.*

Below: Nos. 214 through 230 Bowery today. *Courtesy of Shirley Dluginski.*

established over ninety public education institutions dedicated to African American students.

A familiar site for three generations of Browns and Wheelocks was a three-foot-high slab of stone at the foot of their property on the Bowery, which identified the one-mile mark of Boston Post Road.

In 1775, the postmaster general of the colonies, none other than Benjamin Franklin, took a stagecoach from New York City to Boston to personally measure and select many of the positions where the markers were to be laid. Originally, the first-mile stone marker was located on the Bowery just below Canal Street, and the second was placed at Bowery and Sand Hill Road (Astor Place). The third was located on today's Twenty-fourth Street and Madison Avenue, and they continued about every twenty blocks to the northern tip of Manhattan Island before continuing on through the Bronx, Connecticut, Rhode Island and Massachusetts.

When the new city hall opened in 1812—a full mile north of the original building—the milestones were repositioned accordingly, and marker number one was placed at 214 Bowery at Rivington Street, where it remained for another full century.

222 Bowery

According to *Old Bowery Days: The Chronicles of a Famous Street*, by Alvin Fay Harlow, this was the nineteenth-century site of Arnold's Cider Mill, where a St. Bernard walking on a treadmill crushed apples to the amusement of customers and passersby. This was an era when businessmen had to be creative to compete on a street with numerous theaters, dime museums and other curious amusements. One Bowery clothing store hired actual constables from Ireland to attract Irish customers, another hired live mimes to model clothing as mannequins and at least one storefront showcased a live bear.

In 1885, the first American branch of the Young Men's Christian Association opened here in a new five-story, red brick Queen Anne–style building designed by Bradford Lee Gilbert (who secured the commission with help of YMCA board member Cornelius Vanderbilt II). Gilbert designed the building at a cost of $150,000 in European style in honor of the YMCA's roots, which began in 1848 England.

The interior featured multiple bowling alleys, a large gymnasium and a library and reading rooms and hosted lectures, classes and special events catering to the working class. Membership was only four dollars per year for full use of the facilities, and it had attracted 659 members by 1891.

The YMCA closed its 222 Bowery branch in 1932, and by 1942, the building had been converted to accommodate various manufacturing companies. (Right before the conversion, cubist Fernand Leger lived and worked in the building between 1940 and 1941.)

In 1958, 222 Bowery would go through another change, when it was remodeled into a residential loft space. That same year, painter Mark Rothko was renting an apartment with his family at 102 West Fifty-fourth Street, lured to New York City to create an installation for the Four Seasons restaurant. He found that neighborhood too stuffy and offering no inspiration, so he rented a cavernous loft here in what was the old YMCA gymnasium.

By the early 1960s, artist Wynn Chamberlain had moved into the top-floor loft, which became a popular gathering place for contemporary artists such as Frank O'Hara, Ted Berrigan, Larry Rivers and Andy Warhol, who, in 1964, screened his first movie here to a small private audience that included film pioneer Jonas Mekas. The movie was called *Sleep*, a six-hour-long film featuring an actor sleeping. Apparently at least two guests left after the first hour.

In the leading role of Warhol's *Sleep* was a man named John Giorno, whom Warhol had developed a relationship with in 1962 after meeting at a party. In 1965, Giorno moved into a loft at 222 Bowery, where he founded the alternative record label Giorno Poetry Systems. He went on to experiment with early multimedia/poetry events and produced several popular records, books and videos, including 1972's *Dial-A-Poem Poets* and the 1974 follow-up, *Dial-A-Poem Poets Disconnected*, both double album LPs that showcased the likes of William S. Burroughs (a longtime collaborator), Amiri Baraka, Peter Orlovsky, Ed Sanders and Anne Waldman. New York City born, John Giorno is known today as one of the world's most respected and inspiring living American poets. He also founded the AIDS Treatment Project and still is, in 2011, an active Bowery community member.

From 1975 to 1981, Beat writer William S. Burroughs lived in a second-floor, renovated YMCA locker room at 222 Bowery, which became famously known as "the bunker" because it consisted of three large rooms with no windows. The space had been previously occupied by his lover James Grauerholz and suggested to Burroughs by friend John Giorno. Here, behind three locked gates and a bulletproof door, the carefully reclusive Burroughs entertained the likes of Mick Jagger, Jean Michel Basquiat, Allen Ginsberg, Lou Reed, Patti Smith and noted punk photographer Marcia Resnick.

No. 222 Bowery today. *Courtesy of Shirley Dluginski.*

227 BOWERY

This address is perhaps the only on the Bowery that today houses the same tenants it did a century ago. The Bowery Mission was founded by Reverend Albert Gleason Ruliffson in 1879 and in 1909 opened this chapel at 227 Bowery, where it still plays a leading role in personal, social and spiritual transformation in this city.

The Bowery Mission began offering services in 1880 in a small room Reverend Ruliffson and his supporters rented at 36 Bowery, where it stayed for a period of time before settling at 14 Bowery. In 1895, *Christian Herald* owner Dr. Louis Klopsch purchased the Bowery Mission, saving it from economic hardship and the possibility of closing.

By 1904, plans to construct the Manhattan Bridge had forced the Bowery Mission to find another home. Reverend Ruliffson found this building at 227 Bowery, a former coffin factory and lodging house, and with a paltry $20,000 in renovations, transformed the industrial structure into a sacred space. The new (and present) Bowery Mission opened its doors on November 6, 1909.

One month after the opening, on December 13, 1909, President William H. Taft made an appearance at the mission to address the staff and residents. Though he was late—he didn't arrive until almost 11:00 p.m.—and admittedly oblivious to the culture of the slums, he did praise the great work of the mission. President Taft opened his statement by saying, "My friends, I am just as much surprised at being here as you are to see me here." But he did go on to say, "It is a truly great work to help men over the hard places, to help them at a time when things seem desperate, to show men that there are people who feel with them in their misfortunes and anxious to assist them to get the opportunity which will enable you to achieve something for yourselves."

On November 7, 1919, New York governor Alfred E. Smith spoke at the Bowery Mission's fortieth anniversary. Smith was a hometown hero to many, born and raised in the slums of the Fourth Ward to become one of the twentieth century's greatest social reformers. He understood the unique culture of the Bowery district, stating, "We are here tonight to celebrate forty years of active work on the part of the Bowery Mission, in a section of this city misunderstood throughout the country, in fact, throughout the world."

On July 15, 1920, then Democratic nominee Franklin D. Roosevelt visited the mission while touring the country for support in his vice presidential bid.

He reassured residents in classic Rooseveltese: "I think things are going up, not down. I don't believe in talk of the good old times. These times were never as good as the present. And by the same token, these good times are not as good as those of tomorrow."

But it is not the big names and high-profile speeches that kept the Bowery Mission operating for the last century; it is the people behind the scenes. The volunteers, staff, administration, pastors, counselors, fundraisers, cooks, maintenance men—generations of dedicated individuals whose paths in life brought them to this place. Since day one, the people of the Bowery Mission have devoted countless hours and resources to those in need, and the mission earned its reputation as a champion for the people right away.

During a record snowstorm in the winter of 1909, the Bowery Mission lobbied the City of New York to hire mission workers to help with snow removal. Over 150 men were hired. In 1910, the Bowery Mission lobbied that unemployed Americans in search of work out west be given lower rates on railroad transport. The program was supported by none other than President Taft.

In 1915, J.G. Hallimond, superintendent of the Bowery Mission at the time, sought a pardon from President Woodrow Wilson in 1915 for a former mission worker named Robert Hicks, who was jailed for mailing "unmailable material." The sentence was commuted, and Hicks was released.

In the 1920s, during Prohibition, the Bowery Mission led the way in helping the population adjust to a new ban on alcohol and faced one of its greatest challenges soon after, during the Great Depression, when the mission offered food, shelter and support for an unprecedented number of people suffering from the economic crisis.

More than simply providing day-to-day necessities, the mission looked to brighten the spirits of the unemployed and destitute of the city by offering holiday parties, banquets, motivational speakers, entertainment and even ferry excursions to Long Island—small things to many, but healthy distractions from the reality of everyday life for the people of the day.

The mission's Ed Morgan states: "Recovery is an affair of the heart. We look at recovery of the heart as well as the body and the mind. When the heart is changed, the recovery is permanent." But in 1937, Reverend C.J. St. John perhaps said it best: "The social gospel and the personal gospel—in mission circles we say soup and salvation must go together, and the soup must come first."

235 BOWERY

The London Theatre was opened here on Thanksgiving Day 1876 by Harry Miner and James Donaldson. It was Miner's first theater enterprise, but he sold his half of the business to Donaldson within two years and branched out on his own with Miner's Bowery Theatre at 165–167 Bowery.

Donaldson's London Theatre went on to become an influential variety/burlesque/vaudeville theater featuring some of the country's most celebrated talent. Weber and Fields were regulars; a young Eddie Cantor entered an amateur contest here and was offered a job but was not confident enough to accept.

"The Bowery Girl," Annie Hart, a regular at the London, introduced the song "Annie Rooney" to American audiences in 1890, becoming an overnight sensation. Hart became a star and went on to perform on Broadway well into the 1940s.

In 1894, Lottie Gilson, known as "The Little Magnet," premiered the hit "The Sidewalks of New York" here (known to many by its opening line, "East Side, West Side"), and in 1898, William Claude Dukenfield, better known by his stage name W.C. Fields, made his New York debut at the London Theatre as a juggler.

Donaldson operated the London until the 1890s, when a man named James Henry Curtin took over and ran it until Michael Mintz came along in 1909 and dedicated 235 Bowery to Yiddish theater under the name Lipzen Theatre.

By 1913, the venue had become known as the Variety Theatre, under the management of Morris Heine, and offered vaudeville and motion pictures. Then it became Maiori's Royal Theatre, an Italian playhouse, by 1916.

By 1924, it was called the Caruso Theatre and, by 1926, the Chinese Theatre. In 1930, the building at 235 Bowery was sold, ending almost six decades of theatrical history. Today, this address hosts the New Museum for Contemporary Art, which opened in 2006.

241 BOWERY

At this address once stood a handsome two-story building that housed the depot, ticket booth and early offices of the New York and Harlem Rail Company, incorporated April 25, 1831, and commissioned to lay the first streetcar service in the United States. This pioneering commuter rail operated

Illustration of the first railroad track. *From* 1893 Street Railway Journal.

along the Bowery and Fourth Avenue between city hall and Harlem, with the first section of track work, laid between Prince and Fourteenth Streets, opening on November 14, 1832. Mayor Walter Brown and other city dignitaries took the maiden voyage in a car designed by a local man named John Stephenson.

Hundreds of laborers earning fifty to sixty cents per day began construction of the new rail line in late 1831 at the corner of Prince and Bowery by removing the cobblestone and digging an eighteen- by eighteen-inch trench northward along the route. About every eight feet, three-foot holes were dug to secure stone foundations, which supported long, heavy granite stringers that one-inch-thick iron rails were bolted into.

Each streetcar ran on four wheels and was pulled along the tracks by a team of powerful horses. The coaches had glass windows, cushioned seats, six doors (three on each side) and three non-connecting compartments, which held ten people each (plus a seat atop the car for the driver, which mimicked old omnibus stagecoaches). Once in operation, the rigid construction proved to be too noisy—it was said to be heard from two to three blocks away—so the granite stringers were replaced with pine wood within two years and sold to the city for use as gutter stones.

The first car, named the "John Mason" in honor of the rail company's founder, would run every thirty minutes from 8:00 a.m. until midnight every day except Sunday, for the price of about five cents. The route was extended by small sections at a time, and when it came time to build below Prince Street, the plan was to reach city hall by way of Chatham Square. However, a Sixth Ward alderman named Henry Erben persuaded the company to make a detour along Broome and Centre Streets—conveniently past the good alderman's organ factory at 168 Centre Street.

By 1837, the streetcar line known as the Fourth Avenue Railroad was fully operational between city hall and Eighty-fourth Street, and like the Boston Post Road before it, entire neighborhoods would evolve along the route around the newly created stations.

America's first horse-drawn streetcar was in operation until the end of the century, when the Third Avenue El became a more efficient mode of transportation.

From 1878 until at least 1881, 241 Bowery was home to a well-known concert saloon and brothel named the Sultan Divin, which offered risqué female entertainment, "beautiful bar maids" and private boxes for potential intimate encounters.

By 1910, this address hosted the Fleabag saloon, owned by a formidable gangster named Chick Tricker, whose war with "Big" Jack Zelig made him the target of a drive-by shooting while standing in front of his business on June 4, 1912. Tricker survived by ducking into the building.

The Sunshine Hotel moved into 241 Bowery in 1922 and operated as a lodging house into the next century. For a few dollars a week, men would sleep in rows of individual four- by six-foot, semi-private cubicles referred to as "pigeon coops." In 2001, longtime hotel manager Nate Smith narrated an award-winning radio documentary titled "Sunshine Hotel," produced by David Isay, MacArthur Genius Award winner and creator of Story Corps.

253 BOWERY

In 1893, this address hosted Kahn's Anatomical Museum, a macabre science exhibition/freak show that made its home on the Bowery for over thirty-five years. Depicted by author Felix Riesenberg as "a nightmarish enclave devoted to sexual grotesquery and disease," Kahn's museum was a popular center of amusement, as visitors flocked to see examples of syphilis-ridden faces and deformed genitals.

Kahn's was one of several anatomical museums in Manhattan and one of three operated by the Jordan family, two generations of entrepreneurs/pseudo-scientists with roots in the museum business dating back to 1862, when patriarch Henry Jacob Jordan founded the pioneering Parisian Cabinet of Wonders at 563 Broadway. Jordan, a native Englishman, claimed to have received a doctorate degree from St. Barthomew's Hospital in London, but no sources can confirm that. (Regardless, all "professionals" in the business called themselves "doctors" or "professors.")

Soon after 1854, when Dr. Jordan received a queen's patent for a venereal disease treatment he invented called "Treisemar," the doctor and his four sons made their way to America and began lecturing and publishing articles on subjects pertaining to the science of anatomy and sexual health. By the time Kahn's appeared on the Bowery in 1893, the Jordans had established several similar exhibits in Boston, Philadelphia, San Francisco and New York.

The original location of Kahn's was 708 Broadway, but that was raided and closed down by moral crusaders under the direction of Anthony Comstock in January 1888 along with other local museums, including the Egyptian (138 Bowery), European (81 Bowery) and Parisian (309 Bowery), which kept a row of human skeletons in its storefront window. A *New York Times* article from January 10 of that year featured a headline that read "Revolting Shows Closed." Proprietors were arrested and fined, and truckloads of exhibits were confiscated. Kahn's re-launched a few years later here at 253 Bowery.

Though operating under the guise of science and education, these anatomical museums were nothing more than grafting operations, as none made money purely from admission. Every institution had its way of "working" its guests. Once inside, visitors would be offered a number of opportunities to lose their money on games of chance, anatomical tests or feats of strength. More unscrupulous places would usher individuals or small groups into separate rooms, where "doctors," herbalists, psychics and other seasoned con men would intimidate or cajole people into purchasing products and "services."

Anatomical museums were once respected establishments operated by eminent scholars and noble explorers and were considered precursors to natural history museums. One of the earliest was located on Bowery and Division Street between 1847 and 1849; it showcased such national treasures as the only full mastodon skeleton ever unearthed on American soil at the time. The massive mammoth was excavated by Rembrandt Peale from a farm in the Hudson River Valley in 1801 and put on display at a museum

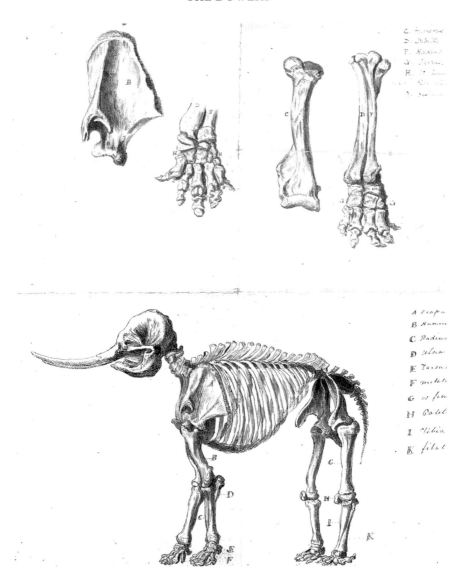

Sketch of a mastodon displayed on the Bowery, by Rembrandt Peale.

in Philadelphia (where Thomas Jefferson attempted to purchase it for his private collection) before being purchased and exhibited on the Bowery a half century later. (A second full mastodon skeleton was uncovered in Jamaica Bay, Queens, in 1858.)

In April 1895, L.J. Jordan, son of Henry Jacob Jordan, was arrested for practicing medicine under a false or assumed name. The younger Jordan also went by the title of "doctor" and had several aliases, including "R.L. Johnstone" and "E.L. Kahn" (thus the name "Kahn's museum"). This arrest and several other brushes with the law did little to curb the Jordan family's shady dealings, and Kahn's Anatomical Museum continued to draw customers with the promise of four-legged chickens, bizarre wax figures, grotesque medical slides and sideshow-worthy performance art.

One unexpected event occurred at Kahn's in 1897, when a man named Rienzi Di Colonna attempted a thirty-day fast as part of a public exhibition. Visitors could pay twenty-five cents to view "Senior Colonna" living in a sealed glass case. About ten days into the exhibition, museum attendants noticed a "very perceptible change in the appearance" of Colonna and alerted doctors later that evening when symptoms had not changed. When doctors arrived, they pronounced that Colonna had been dead for at least two days.

The institution moved three more times—to 294 Bowery in 1898, 312 Bowery in 1905 and Cooper Square in 1915—before finally closing its doors for good in 1920, as one of the last anatomical museums in New York City.

266 Bowery

In the 1830s, a man named S. Clough lived here. He was the publisher of a polarizing book called *The Bible Doctrine of God, Jesus Christ, the Holy Spirit, Atonement, Faith, and Election*, written by Elder William Kinkade and printed across the street by H.R. Piercy at 265 Bowery.

Among the shocking revelations in 1829's *Bible Doctrine* was the suggestion that, based on the laws of nature, God may not be immortal. Kinkade writes, "Seeing all his works perishable, we should naturally be led to think that the author would also die."

In 1844, author Robert Wharton Landis called *The Bible Doctrine* a "wretched tissue of blasphemy," while writer Levi Purviance called it "masterly and hard to refute." Kinkade's book was republished several times and is cited in numerous atheist periodicals and publications.

By the 1950s, 266 Bowery was the headquarters of the John De Salvio Association, named for John De Salvio, a man whose illustrious criminal career spanned over half a century. John De Salvio—aka James De Salvio aka "Jimmy Kelly"—was a politician, nightclub impresario and well-known Bowery gang member, born Giovanni De Salvio at 204 Hester

Street about 1882. He earned the reputation as a brave pugilist as a youth and at age fourteen entered the professional boxing ring, where he was fairly successful as a lightweight for a few years. While still in his teens, De Salvio earned a job as a bouncer at "Nigger Mike's" Chatham Café, where he was introduced to some of New York City's most violent criminals. By the turn of the century, De Salvio found himself running his own gang for hire with close ties to Tim Sullivan and the mighty Eastman Gang. During this time, he went to war with several gangs for control of local gambling and labor-slugging enterprises, during which he was stabbed by the Humpty Jackson Gang and shot by the Five Points Gang, minimally. De Salvio's connections to Tammany and police department officials like Lieutenant Charles Becker (plus a lot of luck) helped him outlast all of his early competition.

De Salvio became proprietor of several Manhattan saloons, including the Folly, a Fourteenth Street criminal dive, and the infamous Mandarin Café in the heart of the "Bloody Angle" of Doyers Street. Deeply rooted in organized crime, his son-in-law was Anthony Carfano, better known as "Lil' Augie Pisano," a career gangster who was once a lieutenant to "The Boss" Giuseppe Masseria and capo in Charles "Lucky" Luciano's organized crime family.

By the 1920s, De Salvio had become one of the most influential community leaders on the Lower East Side, helping Jimmy Walker defeat Mayor Hylan by mobilizing voters in the primary election of 1925. Using his political clout, he formed the John De Salvio Association at 206 Lafayette Street in 1939 and was elected in 1940 as Democratic assemblyman of the Second District of New York. His son, Louis De Salvio, was also elected to State Assembly in the 1940s.

In 1951, De Salvio associate and mob kingpin Frank Costello was questioned about his connection to the De Salvio family in the famous Congressional Organized Crime Hearings in Washington, D.C. Costello responded, "Oh, I might have spoken to Jimmy Kelly...I just don't remember now."

John De Salvio died at sixty-six years old of natural causes on January 4, 1948, but the John De Salvio Association continued well into the 1960s, headquartered out of 266 Bowery. De Salvio Park, on the corner of Mulberry and Spring Streets, was opened in honor of the former assemblyman in 1955.

In the summer of 1975, the rock band Blondie moved into a loft space above a liquor store located at 266 Bowery, where they lived and rehearsed while on the brink of stardom.

267 Bowery

The history of this lot dates back to the 1830s, when an award-winning instrument maker named John Abbott lived here. By the 1850s, it was home to another important assembly room called Early Closing Hall, home to the Carpenters and Plasterers Unions, Real Estate Owners Association and headquarters of Workingman's Union. The Amalgamated Society of Woodworkers was founded here, as was the Order of United Americans Alpha Chapter No. 1, a political association organized to counter the infamous Know-Nothing Party. P.T. Barnum was a member of the Order of United Americans Charter Oak Chapter, which met at 187 Bowery.

In the fall of 1858, the Convention on the Subject of the Bible in the Common Schools was founded here, which fought against a citywide push to take Bible prayers out of the public school system. By the time the convention was formed, thirteen schools in New York City had banned Bible study.

Early Closing Hall lasted until about 1870, and the address went through several tenants over the following decades: furniture sales, lodging houses, factories, warehouses and restaurants, like the one owned by Joseph and Stanislaus Fleischer that was fined $200 in 1911 for selling spoiled food and possessing twelve pounds of "decayed pork," twelve pounds of "diseased liver" and thirty-four gallons of rotten tomatoes.

In the 1940s, a man named Sammy Fuchs unknowingly created a national phenomenon by transforming a grungy Bowery bar at this location into a legendary nightclub called Sammy's Bowery Follies. "Sammy's on the Bowery," as it was simply known, was an enormously popular mid-century entertainment venue/restaurant known for its raucous parties, corny variety shows and odd mix of clientele: theatergoers, celebrities, politicos, tourists, Bowery drunks—revelers from all walks of life rubbing shoulders for one common goal: to party!

In 1934, Sammy Fuchs opened a saloon at this location that originally catered to the derelict population of the district. Fuchs obtained a cabaret license in 1941 after a patron visiting from uptown wandered into the bar and inspired Fuchs to expand his demographics.

Fuchs then hired some former vaudevillian performers, incorporated a Gay Nineties theme and promoted his new club as the "Stork Club of the Bowery." The public ate it up, and Sammy's new Bowery Follies quickly became a mecca for the after-theater crowd, who were treated to singing waiters, romping show tunes, singalongs, cabaret and comedy skits in a true downtown atmosphere. The club's location on the Bowery was part of its appeal; visiting the Bowery at night was thought of as daring, edgy, even dangerous. It was an exciting proposition all around to visit Sammy's, reserved for only the most adventurous and hip.

Being the astute businessman he was, Sammy Fuchs knew exactly what his patrons wanted, so he hired the most outrageous acts he could find and offered Bowery regulars free drinks to stay all night for "atmosphere."

The interior was far from upscale, with a simple décor described as dark and drab with random photos, autographs, quotes and plaques on the walls. A tradition of sawdust on the floor remained from the old saloon days to soak up any spills from the gallons and gallons of alcohol that flowed on a daily basis.

Sammy's was open from 8:00 a.m. until 4:00 a.m. every day. At 8:00 p.m., the entertainment started, and a three-dollar minimum was enforced. (Drinks cost about ninety cents and dinner ran from one to five dollars per entree.) Sammy did not hire cigarette girls, a norm of any big club at the time. Instead, he offered machines that sold cigarettes for one cent apiece.

In fact, nothing about Sammy's Bowery Follies was normal, which contributed to its great success. By the 1940s, several venues attempted to adopt the Sammy's format, one of the first being the Somerset Hotel, which began a Sammy's-style review in its lounge in September 1946, calling it the "Forty-seventh Street Follies." However, none would spark the fascination of the American public like Sammy's, which was featured in several international magazines and guidebooks as a must-see New York experience.

Life magazine published stories about Sammy's several times in the 1940s, most notably "New York Welcomes the U.S. Navy" (November 5, 1945), which features a photo spread of three sailors on leave enjoying an evening on the town at Sammy's; and "Sammy's Bowery Follies" (December 4, 1944), in which many Bowery characters—such as "Queen of the Bowery," Tugboat Ethel—are introduced to the nation with brilliant accompanying photos by Alfred Eisenstaedt, the photographer who shot the iconic V-J in Times Square photos.

The December 4, 1944 article prompted this letter to the editor, which was published the following week, sent in by a St. Paul, Minnesota man: "Never have I read as disgusting and revolting an article in your usually praiseworthy magazine as 'Sammy's Bowery Follies.' Certainly there must be more interesting and educational topics than the Bowery and the dregs of humanity which work in it!"

Samuel Fuchs earned a reputation as a trustworthy, respectable businessman and community leader who spent a large part of his fortune and time helping those less fortunate. Sammy set up a dental clinic for poor neighborhood children, donated food to local missions, offered meals, clothing, haircuts and employment to the destitute and was involved in several community activism initiatives. In one instance, in 1947, as member of the Bowery Improvement Committee, Fuchs fought yet another plan to change the name of the Bowery to something "more dignified," like "Lower Fourth Avenue."

In 1954, Sammy Fuchs heard the story of Anne Myers, a thirty-four-year-old mother who was in desperate need of $400 for an unspecified operation, so she sheepishly robbed the Corn Exchange Bank on Broadway and Ninety-first Street with a toy gun. Mrs. Myers was arrested, charged with robbery and grand larceny and held on $500 bail. Fuchs, a stranger, was moved by the story, so he put up the money to get Myers out of jail, paid for the operation and offered her a job to help get her on her feet.

By the 1950s, Sammy's had become a destination on many a tourist's itinerary and welcomed busloads of patrons at a time. A visit to Sammy's was as important as seeing the Statue of Liberty or Empire State Building, and over 100,000 patrons passed through the doors each year in its post–World War II heyday. Gray Line even offered an all-inclusive nightclub tour that included dinner at the Copa and drinks at Sammy's for $14.95. Surprisingly, the tourist trap reputation did little to dissuade the uptowners and regulars. Midwestern sightseers mingled with rising theater stars and "Bowery bums" alike—united by song, dance, drink and food.

The legend of Sammy's Bowery Follies had seeped into pop culture consciousness, and several theatrical and literary works of the era referenced the venue, such as James Baldwin's 1962 novel *Another Country*, in which a character named Ellis responds to "What brings you down here? [to the Bowery]" with, "I had an uncontrollable urge to see Sammy's Bowery Follies."

An April 1960 *Billboard Magazine* features an album titled *An Evening at Sammy's Bowery Follies* by various artists, and at least one other record was released called *Sammy's Bowery Follies: Songs of Yesterday*.

Sammy Fuchs passed away in April 1969, and his widow, Bessie Fuchs, attempted to keep Sammy's doors open but admittedly did not have the same charisma as her late husband, stating, "Sammy did all the talking. I was just his wife. He mingled with the biggest and the lowest, and they all loved him."

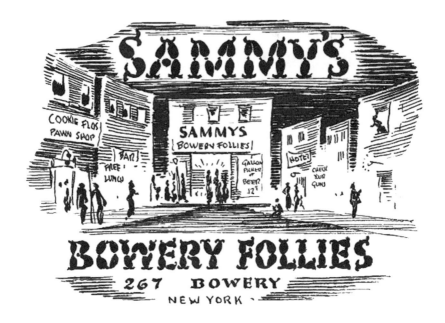

Above: Sammy's dinner card cover. *Courtesy of Lower East Side History Project.*

Below: Sammy's dinner card inside, signed by performers. *Courtesy of Lower East Side History Project.*

Sammy's on the Bowery closed its doors a year and a half later, on September 29, 1970, at 3:00 a.m. Over seven hundred patrons flocked to the club that night to bid farewell, singing old favorites like "Melancholy Baby" and "There's No Business Like Show Business." At the end of night, singer Goldye Shaw said, "I don't know what I'm going to do now. I'm too sad to think—too sad to care."

The closing of Sammy's marked an end to the 150-year-old theater and entertainment tradition on the Bowery. It was a relic even in its heyday, but it was the very last to carry the torch of the "Old Bowery."

The building that hosted Sammy's Bowery Follies was sold to the city in 1970 and was eventually replaced as part of an urban renewal project.

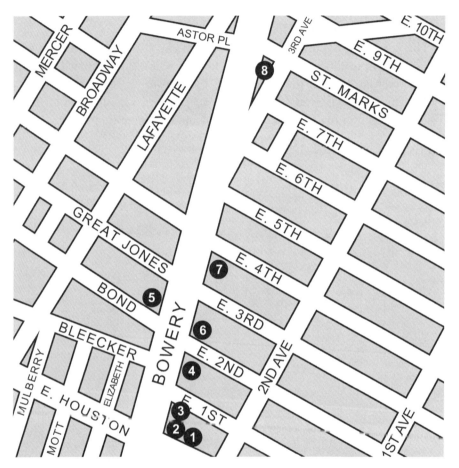

Addresses discussed in this chapter. *Courtesy of Lower East Side History Project.*

Chapter 4

East Houston Street to Astor Place

LIZ CHRISTY GARDEN

This little oasis at the northeast corner of Bowery and East Houston Street is the first community garden in New York City, founded in 1973 and named in honor of local activist and founder Liz Christy, a pioneer in the urban gardening movement of this city.

Liz Christy was an aspiring artist who, along with a few friends, started out by tossing "seed bombs" (balloons and Christmas ornaments filled with seeds, water and fertilizer) into rubble-strewn vacant lots around the Lower East Side, giving life to a neighborhood in significant decay.

By the 1970s, an economic collapse in New York City had greatly affected lower-income areas like South Bronx, the Lower East Side and inner Brooklyn. A sharp increase in unemployment, crime and drug use and a decline of civil services sent many families seeking greener pastures, leaving entire buildings abandoned. Those structures that were not torched were simply demolished by the city, leaving a trail of rubbled lots and uninhabitable brick shells throughout the neighborhood.

Liz Christy's "Green Guerillas," as they called themselves, turned their attention to a debris-filled lot at this corner. Over several backbreaking months, volunteers painstakingly removed rubble, set topsoil and planted vegetables, plants, shrubs and trees. After petitioning the city, the group secured a one-dollar-a-month lease for this property on April 23, 1974. The

Above: Liz Christy inviting a young volunteer into the Bowery Houston community garden and farm in 1974. *Courtesy of founding member Donald Loggins.*

Below: Liz Christy garden, northeast corner of Bowery and East Houston Street today. *Courtesy of Shirley Dluginski.*

Bowery Houston Community Farm and Garden opened that year, inspiring similar projects throughout the Five Boroughs.

The garden was renamed for its founder in 1986 and received a face-lift in 2007 as part of a local development plan. Today, there are over six hundred all-volunteer gardens in the city, with an estimated 10 percent of them on the Lower East Side. The Liz Christy Garden continues to be maintained by community volunteers from all walks of life and has become a popular destination for locals and tourists alike.

291–293 BOWERY

In the mid-1860s, Sixtus Ludwig Kapff founded the Steuben House here, a prominent German social and political hall named after Frederick William, baron von Steuben, a Prussian-born Revolutionary War general and chief of staff in George Washington's administration. Steuben, who wrote the *Revolutionary War Drill Manual* and helped whip the Continental army into shape, became a symbol of adopted patriotism for German Americans of the era, resulting in several buildings, societies, political clubs and streets named in his honor. There was a Steuben Street in Manhattan until 1811 that was located at today's Forty-first Street, and there are still Steuben Streets in many cities, including Brooklyn, Albany, Utica and Jersey City.

According to records, Sixtus Ludwig Kapff was a well-known Württemberg revolutionist who studied law at the University of Tübingen before joining the Freischarelern (mercenaries) at the outbreak of the 1848 German revolution. When his revolutionary pursuits failed, he was forced to flee and landed in New York City, where he became one of the most influential German American community leaders of the era.

When the Civil War began in 1861, one of the very first volunteer regiments in the Union army was organized by the Germans of New York City right here at the Steuben House. Ludwig Kapff served in New York's Seventh Volunteer Regiment, commanded by his brother Eduard Kapff, which saw action in several battles, including the Battle of Fredericksburg in December 1862.

Several high-profile speakers addressed the associations of the Steuben House, including news editor and politician Horace Greeley, who spoke to an enthusiastic crowd of Union loyalists in 1862 "in interest of the Union and a vigorous prosecution of the war," and Roman Jurowski, founder of the first Polish-language newspaper in America, *Echo z. Polski*, in 1863.

On December 21, 1863, a fire gutted both 291 and 293, four and five stories, respectively, and damaged neighboring 295 Bowery, which housed a tobacco factory. Nos. 291 and 293 had to be rebuilt.

The new Steuben House hosted many non-German community and political events, such as the Italian Movement in Support of the War for the Independence and Unity of Italy in June 1866, and began to offer several meetings in English, Yiddish, Italian, Polish and Russian. It had become home to many trade unions, labor organizations and political and community associations of all nationalities.

Kapff sold the buildings in the early 1870s and passed away in New York City on February 20, 1877, at the age of fifty-nine. The Steuben House received a face-lift and was re-launched as the Germania Assembly Rooms by 1874, outfitted with saloons, bowling alleys, meeting rooms and a theater. It was sometimes referred to as Volksgarten. Though not as fancy as many other halls at the time, the Germania was an important community institution shared by all levels of society. By the 1880s, these buildings hosted several German, Italian, French and Polish theater companies, music and shooting societies and social and political organizations.

On September 24, 1878, Adolph Neuendorff was elected conductor of the New York Philharmonic here, beating out notable maestro Leopold Damrosch in votes, 46–29. Neuendorff's run was short-lived, however, and he was relieved of his position in April 1879. One review from the era reads, "He has done his best in the position, but has been of no advantage to the musical character of this society."

The Socialist Labor Party held an event at the Germania on December 5, 1879, entitled "Land and Liberty for the People of Downtrodden Ireland." It was billed as a "Grand Mass Meeting of Sympathy with the Irish People in their Struggle against Tyranny." The event was reported on by the international press, including *Irish World* newspaper.

By 1883, Teatro Italiano occupied the 448-seat theater on the second floor of the building. In February of that year, the theater company gained critical acclaim for its production of *L'Entrata di Garibaldi in Napoli* ("Garibaldi's Entrance into Naples").

Reports from the late 1890s show the building catering to a far more marginal community of gamblers, prostitutes and petty thieves after being sold to John Stemmer in November 1883.

An 1899 report describes a visit to the Germania on October 26, 1899, by two undercover police officers: "We passed through a door off the street and through a long hall and passed the lookout, and we turned to the right and then to the left and into a very large poolroom crowded with men. There were about five hundred men there...We left this place by the Second avenue entrance, at about 4:15 o'clock p.m." The officers reported several illegal activities, such as horse and pool betting, cards, French-made roulette wheels and craps, which the officers referred to as a "negro game" now "generally played" by everyone.

On November 11, 1900, an Italian performance of *Senza Patria* ("Without a Country") was shut down by police as hundreds of anarchists gathered to raise funds for the widow of Gaetano Bresci, a man hanged for the assassination of King Umberto I of Italy. As theatergoers arrived, they were met by a squad of police who instructed the crowd to leave, insisting that the show would not go on. A scuffle ensued, the crowd dispersed and many regrouped around the corner at Mori & Lorenzi's Café at 144 Bleecker Street, which the *New York Times* says "was filled with excited gesticulating Italians" who denounced the police and vowed to even the score "with interest at some future date."

On April 25, 1901, the Committee of Fifteen, organized in 1900 specifically to fight vice in the tenement district, raided the Volksgarten, armed with warrants for two of its managers, Henry and George Stall. A street-wise bouncer at McGurk's next door noticed a detective snooping around the front of 291–293 and alerted its staff that a raid was imminent. A bartender named Anthony Heffert fled out the back door on Second Avenue and down East Houston Street, but police caught up with him. Several people were arrested, including George Stall, and charged with aiding, keeping and abetting a disorderly house.

On November 23, 1901, Captain James Churchill of the Fifth Street Station, after just a week on the job, decided to shake things up and pay a visit to the biggest gambling den in his district, 291–293 Bowery. The good captain told proprietor John Stimmel, "There is gambling going on here, there is a poolroom, all I have to say is it has to stop." Churchill later said that there were 280 men in the room and he was threatened not to interfere.

Captain Churchill was not intimidated and returned just a few days later to find an oak door "six times as thick as a regular door" and secured by "three great bolts" leading to the main hall—which were not present on the prior visit—so he had it smashed to pieces with axes and crowbars. Once inside, they encountered five more obstacles that had to be breached, and by the time they raided the main room it was empty. Hundreds escaped through the rear of the building on Second Avenue. (You would think they would have caught on to that route by this time.)

In June 1902, Captain Churchill was called as a witness in the trial of ex–police inspector Adam A. Cross, who was facing charges of neglect of duty and charges unbecoming of an officer for allowing gambling to go on under his watch. Churchill was first assigned to his post at the East Fifth Street Station with instructions to "clear up the disorder" left by the previous captain, who was dismissed from the force. Needless to say, Churchill's noble efforts were not welcome by many. As soon as he took up his post, he was passed a "quiet tip" that he'd better keep his hands off the gambling enterprise at the Germania. It was, after all, financially backed by Frank Farell, a business partner of ex–police chief William Stephen Devery. (The two would purchase a Baltimore, Maryland baseball team and move it to New York City in 1903. This team would become the New York Yankees.) When Churchill dismissed the warnings and busted up the club in 1901, Chief Devery ordered Inspector Cross to lead bogus raids in Churchill's district, which led to charges and a dismissal from his post as captain.

Inspector Adam A. Cross had previously been on trial several times, most notably charged with neglect of duty in connection with the riot at a funeral for Rabbi Jacob Joseph on Grand Street in July 1902 for failure to provide sufficient escort, making misleading statements and allowing policemen to club citizens. He was acquitted in every case.

It looks like Captain Churchill's valiant efforts were not in vain; John Stimmel sold the buildings in June 1902 for $150,000, and by 1904, a mission named Hadley Hall took over the premises, where it served tens of thousands of homeless and jobless men and women over the following three decades. Hadley Hall was opened by friends of Samuel Hopkins Hadley shortly after his death. Hadley was a popular "converted drunkard" turned reformer who made a name for himself as superintendent of the Water Street Mission, where he helped possibly thousands of men denounce alcohol in the name of God.

The superintendent of Hadley Hall was former bartender and ex-convict Reverend John Callahan, who, along with his wife, Mary Johnson Callahan, served supper and provided religious services for hundreds of men and women a day. In its heyday, Hadley Hall served over 1,300 Christmas dinners and allowed over two hundred men to take shelter in the mission hall between 7:30 p.m. and 5:00 a.m. daily.

Reverend Callahan, who was also chaplain of the redoubtable Tombs Prison, became a respectable member of the community and garnered much praise and support for his work. In 1912, President William Taft sent Reverend Callahan a letter of support and personal check for $100 as part of a fundraiser to save his home in Scarsdale, New York.

By the 1940s and '50s, 291–293 had suffered much the same fate as the rest of the Bowery district—it became a mixed-use factory, wholesaler and lodging house for most of the century until it was demolished in 2006 as part of the Cooper Square Redevelopment Plan, which also claimed the structure at 295 Bowery.

295 Bowery

This address has hosted an interesting assortment of tenants throughout the years. In 1840, it was Abel S. Smith's Country Pork Store; by 1856, a barbershop run by William Barr; by 1860, a tobacco manufacturer; and between 1871 and 1873, it was home to the German Pilgrim Lodge No. 20 of the Free and Accepted Masons. In 1886, St. David's Benefit Society (est. 1835) was here, a lodging house and mutual aid society for "Welshman and their decedents."

Between 1895 and 1902, a man named John McGurk operated a saloon at 295 Bowery that was a haven for local thugs, petty thieves, prostitutes, gamblers, gangsters, rowdy sailors, the curious and the brave—your standard turn-of-the-century Bowery dive, actually. However, this venue is most well known for a bizarre tradition that developed in its back room as early as 1897.

Originally named McGurk's after its owner, the venue is best known as "Suicide Hall"—a moniker earned after many people attempted to take their lives in its back room (several were successful). The method of choice was carbolic acid and a shot of whiskey. Why they chose McGurk's of all places, nobody knows, but the proprietor took full advantage of the publicity and officially changed the name to Suicide Hall in 1899. The burly staff were specially trained to deal with individuals who chose McGurk's for their final toast—they would pick them up and throw them on the curb before they died so the police would not interrupt business for an investigation.

Suicide Hall was shut down by authorities in February 1902. By the very next year, there were several retail businesses occupying the premises: Wollin & Goldstein office supplies; Tartar, Billinsky & Co. looking glasses; and Lipman & Silberstien cloth hats and caps.

A fire gutted the upper three floors on April 6, 1922, when it was home to Brooklyn Jobbing House. According to the *New York Times*, sparks from the fire threatened Knickerbocker Warehouse a block away at 28 Second Avenue, which firefighters had to dampen to keep from burning. (This warehouse

Lubarsky Hardware, 295 Bowery, circa 1928—Joseph, Pearl and Nathan Lubarsky. *Courtesy of Sylvia Stella.*

held most of the alcohol confiscated in Manhattan and Brooklyn during Prohibition—up to $15 million worth.)

Lubarsky's Hardware and the Liberty Hotel lasted here throughout the late 1920s and '30s, and the building remained a mixed-use property until 1966, when local artists such as Kate Millet transferred 295 Bowery into an artists' residence, as it would remain for close to forty years.

In 2006, after a three-year battle, Millet and her neighbors were relocated to make way for the nine-story, two-hundred-plus-unit apartment building/retail space you see today.

315 Bowery

In 1969, an ex-marine named Hilly Crystal took over operations of a dive bar at this location. This event would unknowingly contribute to music history.

Crystal was a manager at the Village Vanguard between 1959 and 1964, where he worked with performers like Miles Davis and Lenny Bruce before

Hilly Crystal outside of CBGB in 1977. *Courtesy of GOLDIS.*

Outside of CBGB in 1977. *Courtesy of GOLDIS.*

opening a bar on West Ninth Street in 1966, simply known as "Hilly's." That same year, he partnered with concert promoter Ron Delsner to produce concerts in Central Park. Crystal soon opened a second location on Thirteenth Street before finding this location in 1969, which was referred to as "Hilly's on the Bowery." In 1973, Crystal changed the name to CBGB & OMFUG, which stands for "Country, Blue Grass & Blues and Other Music for Uplifting Gormandizers."

CBGB would go on to pioneer the genre known as "punk rock" and launch the careers of Blondie, the Ramones, Talking Heads, Patti Smith and numerous other artists.

The iconic club closed its doors on October 15, 2006, after a performance by Patti Smith and Lenny Kaye, due to a rent dispute. Today, 315 Bowery hosts a designer clothing store.

330 BOWERY

This rare, French Second Empire–style, cast-iron building, designed by architect Henry Engelbert, was built between 1873 and 1874 for the Bond Street Savings Bank. In 1879, it became known as the German Exchange Bank (organized 1872), which by 1919 had expanded with branch offices at nos. 1196 and 321 Broadway. In 1920, the institution changed its name to Commercial Exchange Bank, which it remained for several more years.

No. 330 Bowery today. *Courtesy of Shirley Dluginski.*

In 1963, theater producer Honey Waldman renovated the building into the 196-seat off-off-Broadway Bouwerie Lane Theatre, which opened on November 2 of that year with a critically acclaimed production of *The Immoralist* starring Frank Langella.

The Jean Cocteau Repertory Company, founded around the corner at 43 Bond Street in 1971 by director Eve Adamson, called the Bouwerie Lane Theatre home between 1974 and 2007 before moving on and changing its name to the Exchange.

Today, the building is a mixed-use residential and commercial space, with a clothing store occupying the ground floor.

341 Bowery

This was the address of the "Upper" police station and Fifth District Court, established in 1832. It tried cases from the Ninth, Eleventh, Fifteenth and Seventeenth Wards of Lower Manhattan. (The "Lower" police court was located at the Tombs Prison, north of city hall.)

Dry Dock Savings Bank was incorporated here in 1848 and served the community for over a century, until the 1960s. On June 16, 1932, a unique five-dollar bill (No. B50522787, for the record) was innocently deposited here by a woman named Martha Sohn. It turns out that the bill was being tracked by authorities because it had been supplied to the kidnappers of the Lindbergh baby as part of a ransom request. An investigation into the woman who made the deposit yielded no results.

By the 1970s, a gas station occupied this lot until a $20 million development in 2003 produced the current building.

357 Bowery

This handsome red brick and cast-iron, four-story, pitched-roof structure was built in 1870 for the Germania Fire Insurance Company, which was founded in 1859. As the name suggests, the company was operated by, and devoted to, the prospering central European population of Kleindeutschland.

Industrial tenants took over by the turn of the century, and starting in 1929, a barber- and beauty shop supply manufacturer made a forty-year

No. 357 Bowery today.
Courtesy of Shirley Dluginski.

run at this address until Good Earth Pottery and several residents moved in during the 1970s.

No. 357 Bowery was landmarked in 2009, and today the building is entirely residential.

COOPER UNION

This landmark building was erected in 1859 as an educational institution, political hall and public library for the Cooper Union for the Advancement of Science and Art, the first full-scholarship school dedicated to higher education in the country.

Beyond turning out some of America's brightest architects and engineers over the last century and a half, Cooper Union has hosted some truly groundbreaking history in its Great Hall. It is where Abe Lincoln gave his celebrated "Right Makes Might" speech in 1860, securing his bid for presidency; where seventeen-year-old Clara Lemlich Shavelson inspired the "Uprising of 20,000" in 1909, leading to sweeping labor reforms; where the earliest women's suffrage and NAACP meetings were held and the American Red Cross was founded; and where countless notable speakers appeared, from Ulysses S. Grant and Theodore Roosevelt to Bill Clinton and Barack Obama.

The man behind Cooper Union was inventor and philanthropist Peter Cooper, a man with no formal education whose passion for engineering made him one of the most revered and successful entrepreneurs in the country.

Cooper was born the fifth of nine children in New York City on February 12, 1791, to John Cooper, Revolutionary War veteran and hat maker, and Margaret Campbell-Cooper, who served as a quartermaster for the Continental army. Though not impoverished, the family was struggling; they named Peter after the apostle, hoping "the boy would come to something."

Young Cooper opted out of an education after only one year and would accompany his father to the family's hat shop on today's Water Street, where he would learn the trade inside and out. By the time Peter was fifteen, his father had financial difficulties and had to move his business (and family) several times, finally settling in the town of Newburg in upstate New York.

With his father's consent, seventeen-year-old Peter Cooper returned to New York City on his own with ten dollars in his pocket (all of which he foolishly lost in a lottery) and sought employment. After many rejections, he came upon a carriage shop on the corner of Broadway and Chambers Street that hired him as an apprentice for twenty-five dollars a week plus boarding. Instead of partaking in social activities with other apprentices, Cooper spent nights and weekends reading, studying with a private tutor (who taught him basic arithmetic) and experimenting with the design of several mechanical devices.

Within just a few years, Cooper patented a cloth-shearing machine, which was a commercial success. He used his earnings to pay off his struggling family's debts and save them from bankruptcy; however, the industry changed by 1815, and his invention was no longer valued. Cooper tried his hand in various businesses before purchasing a grocery store in 1816 on the north side of today's Astor Place between Third and Fourth Avenues (directly across the street from where Cooper Union stands now). Located on the edge of Bowery Village along Boston Post Road, Cooper's store saw steady business.

The estate also included six lots that he developed as the city grew, adding to Cooper's success and status.

By 1821, Cooper had sold his grocery business and invested his life savings in a glue factory property on Fourth Avenue between Thirty-first and Thirty-fourth Streets, which was nearby the New Bull's Head cattle market. Cooper experimented with the remains of livestock to develop glues, cements and gelatins—products that would make him a fortune.

In 1828, Cooper purchased three thousand acres of land near Baltimore, Maryland, for $105,000, under the assumption that the Baltimore & Ohio Railroad was going to be built through the area and the value of the property would increase. While excavating the land, a deposit of iron ore was discovered, which led Cooper to experiment with metallurgy—and the invention of America's first steam engine locomotive, the "Tom Thumb."

As a tribute to Cooper's resourcefulness, the Tom Thumb came about only after hearing that the promised B&O Railroad might not be realized due to technical complications. Instead of losing his investment, Cooper simply invented a machine that solved the problem.

Cooper sold his Maryland property by the 1830s and continued to manufacture glues and iron, going on to invent materials that would change the future of architecture.

He became politically active and was appointed as commissioner of the Public School Society (precursor to the Board of Education) in 1839. In 1840, Cooper was elected to the Board of Aldermen for the Seventeenth Ward, where he championed for teachers, policemen, firemen and small business owners. He became president of the New York, Newfoundland and London Telegraph Company in 1854, later known as the Atlantic Telegraph Company, which laid the first cable across the Atlantic Ocean.

These are just a few of Peter Cooper's professional achievements; however, his greatest satisfaction came with the completion of the Cooper Union in the spring of 1859, built under Cooper's strict supervision on his old property along the Bowery. It was his life's dream to provide individuals, regardless of class, a fair opportunity at an education, which the new institution provided at no cost.

In a speech in July of that year, Cooper stated, "This building has scarcely been absent from my thoughts for a single day for nearly thirty years. I have labored for it, by night and by day, with an intensity of desire that can never be explained."

Today, Cooper Union remains a full-scholarship school, offering one of the most respected arts and sciences programs in the country.

Bibliography

Adler, Jacob P., and Lulla Rosenfeld. *Jacob Adler: A Life on the Stage: A Memoir.* N.p.: Hal Leonard Corporation, 2001.

Aleandri, Emelise. *The Italian-American Immigrant Theatre of New York City.* Charleston, SC: Arcadia Publishing, 1999.

———. *Little Italy.* Charleston, SC: Arcadia Publishing, 2002.

Anbinder, Tyler. *Five Points: The 19th-Century New York City Neighborhood that Invented Tap Dance, Stole Elections, and Became the World's Most Notorious Slum.* New York: Simon and Schuster, 2001.

Bank, Rosemarie K. *Theatre Culture in America, 1825–1860.* New York: Cambridge University Press, 1997.

Barnum, Phineas Taylor. *The Life of P.T. Barnum: Written by Himself.* New York: Redfield, 1855.

Barry, Gerald J. *The Sailors' Snug Harbor: A History, 1801–2001.* New York: Fordham University Press, 2000.

Beach, Wooster. *A Treatise on Anatomy, Physiology, and Health: Designed for Students, Schools, and Popular Use.* New York: Beach, 1847.

Beck, Louis Joseph. *New York's Chinatown: An Historical Presentation of Its People and Places.* New York: Bohemia, 1898.

Bolton, Reginald Pelham. *Indian Paths in the Great Metropolis.* New York: Museum of the American Indian, 1922.

Brownell, Henry Howard. *The Discoverers, Pioneers, and Settlers of North and South America.* New York: American Subscription, 1856.

Burrows, Edwin G., and Mike Wallace. *Gotham: A History of New York City to 1898.* New York: Oxford University Press, 2000.

Campbell, Helen, and Thomas Wallace Knox. *Darkness and Daylight: Or, Lights and Shadows of New York Life*. Hartford, CT: A.D. Worthington, 1892.

Chernow, Ron. *Alexander Hamilton*. New York: Penguin, 2005.

Connors, Chuck. *Bowery Life*. New York: R.K. Fox, 1904.

Cozzens, Issachar. *A Geological History of Manhattan or New York Island*. New York: W.E. Dean, 1843.

Ellet, Elizabeth Fries. *Domestic History of the American Revolution*. New York: Baker and Scribner, 1850.

Hamilton, Marybeth. *When I'm Bad, I'm Better: Mae West, Sex, and American Entertainment*. Berkeley: University of California Press, 1997.

Harlow, Alvin Fay. *Old Bowery Days: The Chronicles of a Famous Street*. New York: D. Appleton, 1931.

Haswell, Charles Haynes. *Reminiscences of an Octogenarian of the City of New York: 1816 to 1860*. New York: Harper & Brothers, 1896.

Hemstreet, Charles. *Nooks & Corners of Old New York*. New York: Charles Scribner's sons, 1899.

Hodges, Graham Russell. *Root & Branch: African Americans in New York & East Jersey, 1613–1863*. Chapel Hill: University of North Carolina Press, 1999.

Homberger, Eric. *The Historical Atlas of New York City: A Visual Celebration of Nearly 400 Years of New York City's History*. New York: Macmillan, 2005.

Horton, William Ellis. *Driftwood of the Stage*. Detroit, MI: Winn & Hammond, 1904.

Irving, Washington. *A History of New York from the Beginning of the World to the End of the Dutch Dynasty*. New York: G.P. Putnam's Sons, 1889.

Johnston, Henry Phelps. *The Campaign of 1776 around New York and Brooklyn*. New York: Long Island Historical Society, 1878.

Jones, Thomas. *History of New York during the Revolutionary War: And of the Leading Events in the Other Colonies at that Period*. New York: New-York Historical Society, 1879.

Lester, Charles Edwards. *Lester's History of the United States: Illustrated in Its Five Great Periods: Colonization, Consolidation, Development, Achievement, Advancement*. Vol. 1. New York: P.F. Collier, 1883.

Lin, Jan. *Reconstructing Chinatown: Ethnic Enclave, Global Change*. Minneapolis: University of Minnesota Press, 1998.

Mariano, John Horace. *The Italian Contribution to American Democracy*. Boston: Christopher Publishing House, 1921.

McLean, Albert F. *American Vaudeville as Ritual*. Lexington: University of Kentucky Press, 1965.

Moss, Frank, and Charles Henry Parkhurst. *The American Metropolis: From Knickerbocker Days to the Present Time; New York City Life in All Its Various Phases*. New York: P.F. Collier, 1897.

Mushabac, Jane, and Angela Wigan. *A Short and Remarkable History of New York City. Museum of the City of New York*. New York: Fordham University Press, 1999.

Nash, George W., and Hopper Striker Mott. *Historical Guide to the City of New York*. New York: Frederick A. Stokes, 1915.

Ostrow, Daniel, and Mary Sham. *Manhattan's Chinatown*. Charleston, SC: Arcadia Publishing, 2008.

Pound, Arthur. *The Golden Earth: The Story of Manhattan's Landed Wealth*. Norwood, MA: Norwood Press, 1935.

Pritchard, Evan T. *Native New Yorkers: The Legacy of the Algonquin People of New York*. San Francisco: Council Oak Books, 2002.

Rider, Fremont. *Rider's New York City and Vicinity, Including Newark, Yonkers and Jersey City*. New York: H. Holt and Company, 1916.

Sanderson, Eric W., and Markley Boyer. *Mannahatta: A Natural History of New York City*. New York: Abrams, 2009.

Sappol, Michael. *A Traffic of Dead Bodies: Anatomy and Embodied Social Identity in Nineteenth-Century America*. Princeton, NJ: Princeton University Press, 2002.

Shorto, Russell. *The Island at the Center of the World*. New York: Random House, 2005.

Shteir, Rachel. *Striptease: The Untold History of the Girlie Show*. New York: Oxford University Press, 2004.

Tchen, John Kuo Wei. *New York Before Chinatown: Orientalism and the Shaping of American Culture, 1776–1882*. Baltimore, MD: Johns Hopkins University Press, 2001.

Todd, Charles Burr. *A Brief History of the City of New York*. New York: American Book Company, 1899.

Trager, James. *The New York Chronology: The Ultimate Compendium of Events, People, and Anecdotes from the Dutch to the Present*. New York: HarperCollins, 2004.

Ward, Geoffrey C., Ken Burns and Ric Burns. *The Civil War*. New York: Random House, 1994.

Zhou, Min. *Chinatown: The Socioeconomic Potential of an Urban Enclave*. Philadelphia: Temple University Press, 1995.

"The Bowery"

A song from the musical A Trip to Chinatown,
lyrics by Charles H. Hoyt, 1891

Oh! the night that I struck New York,
I went out for a quiet walk.
Folks who are on to the city say,
Better by far that I took Broadway.

But I was out to enjoy the sights,
There was the Bow'ry a blaze with lights;
I had one of the devil's own nights,
I'll never go there any more!

The Bow'ry, the Bow'ry!
They say such things,
And they do strange things
On the Bow'ry!
The Bow'ry!
I'll never go there any more!

I had walked but a block or two,
When up came a fellow and me he knew;
Then a policeman came walking by
Chased him away, and I ask'd him, "Why?"
"Wasn't he pulling your leg?" said he;
Said I: "He never laid hands on me!"
"Get off the Bow'ry, you, yep!" said he.
I'll never go there any more!

The Bow'ry, the Bow'ry!
They say such things,
And they do strange things
On the Bow'ry!
The Bow'ry!
I'll never go there any more!

Then I went into an auction store,
I never saw any thieves before.
First he sold me a pair of socks,
Then said he, "How much for the box?"

Someone said "two dollars!" I said
    "three!"
He emptied the box and he gave it to me,
"I told you the box, not the socks," said
    he.
I'll never go there any more!

The Bow'ry, the Bow'ry!
They say such things,
And they do strange things
On the Bow'ry!
The Bow'ry!
I'll never go there any more!

I went into a concert hall,
I didn't have a good time at all.
Just the minute that I sat down
Girls began singing "New Goon in Town."

I got up mad, and I spoke out free,
"Somebody put that man out," said she;
A man called a bouncer attended to me,
I'll never go there any more!

The Bow'ry, the Bow'ry!
They say such things,
And they do strange things
On the Bow'ry!
The Bow'ry!
I'll never go there any more!

I went into a barber shop,
He talk'd till I thought he'd never stop.
I: "Cut it short," he misunderstood,
Clipp'd down my hair just as close as he
    could.

He shaved with a razor that scratched
    like a pin,
Took off my whiskers and most of my
    chin.
That was the worst scrape I ever got in,
I'll never go there any more!

The Bow'ry, the Bow'ry!
They say such things,
And they do strange things
On the Bow'ry!
The Bow'ry!
I'll never go there any more!

I struck a place that they called a "dive,"
I was in luck to get out alive.
When the policeman had heard my woes,
Saw my black eyes and my battered nose;

"You've been held up!" said the copper,
    "Fly!"
"No, sir, but I've been knock'd down!"
    said I;
Then he laughed, tho' I couldn't see why,
I'll never go there any more!

The Bow'ry, the Bow'ry!
They say such things,
And they do strange things
On the Bow'ry!
The Bow'ry!
I'll never go there any more!

About the Author

E ric Ferarra is the founder and executive director of the Lower East Side History project, an award-winning nonprofit research organization. He also founded the East Village Visitor Center, as well as the first museum in America dedicated to gansterism. Ferrara is a popular public speaker, sits on a number of local boards and has consulted on numerous movie and television projects.

A true product of the Lower East Side melting pot, Ferrara's ancestors arrived to New York City from Sicily (1880s), Ukraine (1909), Russia (1917) and Naples (1940s.) He is a fourth-generation native New Yorker and dedicated community activist. This is his second title as an author for The History Press.